"My Ole Miss teammate J[...] his teammate Chucky Mullins. Although Chucky and I never played together, Jody has helped me to better understand and appreciate Chucky's impact upon so many. I recommend this read to everyone who has a love for Ole Miss or Chucky Mullins. I think you will find it to be an inspiration"

—*Cooper Manning, Former Football Player, Ole Miss Rebels*

"My former player Jody Hill has written a firsthand account of the life and legacy of our beloved Chucky Mullins. This is not hearsay, but the direct feelings offered by family, friends, and teammates. Every Rebel needs to read this. He got it right!"

—*Billy Brewer, Former Head Football Coach, Ole Miss Rebels*

"Chucky Mullins injury and death instantly had a lasting and profound effect on the University of Mississippi football program. Chucky Mullins life, though, has changed Ole Miss, and our essence, forever. This is a well written accolade of this once in a generation man and his multi-generational legacy."

—*Bill Courtney, Author,* **AGAINST THE GRAIN**, *he was also the subject of the 2011 Oscar winning documentary* **UNDEFEATED**

"An amazing book about an amazing man—Chucky Mullins. 38 was a man of immense COURAGE and through all of his battles, he found a reason to SMILE! Thank you, Jody, for bringing Chucky Mullins into my life. He continues to inspire, 25 years after his passing. Wish I had known him. But wait, I feel as though I do now and I'm a better person for having read 38. Thank you for writing these 38 stories and sharing them with me and the world. Chucky's legacy is alive and will continue to inspire millions of people. What a man! What a legacy!"

—*Margaret King, Co-Author,* Y'ALL TWINS?, WHICH IS WHICH? *and* OUR JOSEPHINE

38

38

the

CHUCKY MULLINS EFFECT

by JODY HILL

DEEDS PUBLISHING | ATLANTA

Published by Deeds Publishing
Marietta, GA
www.deedspublishing.com

Library of Congress Cataloging-in-Publications Data is available upon request.

ISBN 978-1-941165-32-4

Books are available in quantity for promotional or premium use. For information, write Deeds Publishing, PO Box 682212, Marietta, GA 30068 or info@deedspublishing.com.

First Edition

10 9 8 7 6 5 4 3 2

CONTENTS

INTRODUCTION

WE HAVE BEEN ASKED ON SEVERAL OCCASIONS TO SHARE THE DE-
tails of our life with Chucky Mullins. We have always been hesitant
to respond to those requests. Our main concern is that Chucky be
remembered in a manner that is accurate to the wonderful person
he was.

Chucky's Ole Miss teammate Jody Hill approached us about
his idea of writing a book about Chucky in the fall of 2012. We
explained to Jody our normal reservations because it is so important that Chucky's life be celebrated in the right way. Through
much discussion with Jody we reached a peace of mind that he had
Chucky's best interest in mind for his book idea.

Thus we made the decision to partner with Jody to share Chucky
more intimately with the larger world. In addition to our story, we
understand Chucky was beloved by family, teammates, coaches,
and friends, so we pointed Jody in the direction of some other
meaningful people in Chucky's life.

We were fortunate enough to be blessed by sharing our lives
with Chucky. We believe this book will be a blessing to many others as they learn more about this very special person. Chucky has
encouraged many through his motto: "Never Quit." We pray that
each one who reads this book will also be inspired by Chucky's
story.

Karen's sister Linda and her husband Harlan "Peaches" Winston
were our anchors of support throughout Chucky's injury. They
made weekly trips to Memphis, Birmingham and Mississippi,
along with their small kids, to give their love to our family.

We are also grateful for the tireless efforts of Mrs. Hattie Winston. She took care of any needs we had in Russellville while we lived in Mississippi. After Chucky's death she maintained his grave with care and affection.

While staying in Memphis for the months after Chucky's injury, Rose Marie Blake gave the love to our family that we deeply needed. We will never forget how she embraced us and made us feel like we were part of her family.

Carver and Karen Phillips
Guardians of Chucky Mullins

PROLOGUE

"I'm afraid to go to sleep…because I might not wake up."

THESE WORDS WERE UTTERED BY CHUCKY MULLINS HOURS AFTER he sustained a football injury that forever incapacitated his body.

On October 28, 1989, Chucky Mullins was a redshirt freshman defensive back from Russellville, Alabama, playing for the Ole Miss Rebels football team in their homecoming game against Vanderbilt University. In the first quarter of competition Chucky slammed into a Vandy receiver, separating him from the ball. It was a touchdown-saving hit. But as Chucky launched himself like a human torpedo, there was also an explosion in his neck. Chucky destroyed four vertebrae in his spinal column and was instantly paralyzed from the neck down.

Ole Miss Head Athletic Trainer Leroy Mullins traveled with his injured player by ambulance to the Baptist Memorial Hospital in Memphis, Tennessee. He sat by Chucky's side until his guardians, Carver and Karen Phillips, arrived from their home in Russellville, Alabama, at three o'clock in the morning. As Leroy was preparing to leave in the early morning hours, Chucky shared his fear of not waking up.

Leroy asked, "Chucky, do you believe that there is something beyond this life?"

Chucky said, "Yes, I am a Christian, and I believe I will go to heaven."

Leroy did not have to say he was also a Christian. He had been exemplifying his faith for the entire year that Chucky had known him. "Chucky, I know you're scared, but if you don't wake up you are gonna be in a much better place than this world. Try to get some rest, son. I will see you soon." Leroy truly believed the words he had spoken to Chucky. He would see Chucky soon—if not on this earth, then certainly in heaven.

Chucky made that journey to heaven some eighteen months later, on May 6, 1991.

Even today, more than two decades later, Leroy Mullins can vividly recount that first evening he spent at Chucky's side. But what was even more amazing to Leroy was Chucky's transformation during the last eighteen months of life. He saw Chucky mature spiritually, in a manner not of this world.

The retired trainer's voice takes on a mystical tone as he states, "I believe that as the months passed after his injury, Chucky grew in a way to no longer fear death. Near the end of his life, he had started giving things away that were precious to him. Maybe he somehow knew that his time on earth was drawing to an end."

I first met Chucky Mullins in the summer of 1988. He and I were members of the freshmen class of the Ole Miss Rebels football team, but more than a teammate, Chucky embraced me as a friend. His constant smile was like a welcome light to me and to everyone he met. Like the other people you will meet in this book, my life continues to be enriched by the friendship I shared with Chucky Mullins.

In the year 2000, I felt a call to turn my life in a different direction. I left a lucrative job in a family-owned business to become a pastor in the Cumberland Presbyterian Church of Memphis, Tennessee. More than a decade after his injury my life was still being influenced by Chucky—he made me want to do more than make a living in this world—he made me want to change the world for the better. Perhaps, most importantly, he taught me that even when life frowns upon us, we can still respond with a *smile*.

And that beaming smile, that gracious and spiritual response to catastrophe, is what inspired me to write his story. But this is not a book about a dedicated athlete whose life was cut short by tragedy. Instead, it's a testament to how Chucky moved the world from his motionless state. While portions present a biographical look at Chucky's life, that is not the sole purpose of this work. I have also included an intimate glimpse into the lives of family, friends, and teammates who continue to be touched by the *Chucky Mullins Effect*.

It's been 25 years since the horrific accident that forever altered Chucky Mullins, as well as the University of Mississippi, and the millions of people who heard his courageous story. Yet, without lifting a finger, he is still sculpting a more full existence in the lives of those who witness the courage of 38.

It is my prayer that this work will bring glory to God, who has welcomed Chucky into his heavenly home, and who has graciously walked with me throughout this pilgrimage. In addition, I hope that all who glean here a taste of Chucky's fruitful effect upon his world will be nourished by the spirit of 38.

Jody Hill
June 23, 2014

1 : IMPACT

IN THE SPRING OF 1980, ED WANTED TO CHRISTEN HIS NEWBORN son with an Ole Miss-themed name. Not an easy task when the last half of that formula has the un-Southern ring of Meisenheimer. The name reflected Ed's German descent and was not so foreign in his home state of Illinois.

He fell in love with a young lady from Selmer, Tennessee named Molly Webb while they attended the University of Mississippi, and would ask her to be his wife. Besides their passion for one another, the two became enthralled with Ole Miss Football and the prolific skills of legendary quarterback Archie Manning. This humble young man had mesmerized college football just ten years prior and the Meisenheimers were still feeling the *impact*.

This icon of Ole Miss graced the cover of *Sports Illustrated* on September 14, 1970, and William F. Reed described him this way, "He has red hair, freckles, and a rather prominent nose, and his sturdy young face always seems to reflect a certain quality of sadness and rural innocence."

So, of course, Ed thought "Archie" was the perfect name for this child of Ole Miss alumni who was also graced with glowing strawberry-blond hair. But Molly would have nothing of it, no matter how much she embraced Ed's love for Ole Miss. Although the redhead from Drew, Mississippi, was safe from a direct namesake on this occasion, his hometown sounded like a perfect fit. Thus, the compromise was complete, and Drew Meisenheimer was so named on May 7, 1980.

By his ninth birthday, Drew had made countless family trips to Oxford from their home in Memphis, Tennessee, giving birth to his own love for the Rebels. On Oct 28, 1989, Drew traveled with his dad to the Ole Miss Homecoming game against the Vanderbilt Commodores. Molly and little brother, Tyler, were preoccupied with other events, so this would be a guy trip for the two oldest men of the house. Drew envisioned a special day in his mind: he could eat all the hotdogs he wanted, he didn't have to worry with the horror of having to leave the game early because six-year-old Tyler "got tired," and it would surely be a win because they were playing Vandy. Drew's premonition would indeed prove accurate. It most certainly became a day that *impacted* the young family for the rest of their lives.

Late in the first quarter, the Commodores were driving to score and there was a pass attempt to their star running back, Brad Gaines. But just as the pass arrived, a pass defender wearing number 38 for the Rebels made *impact*. The ball was dislodged, and it was a touchdown-saving play. Drew jumped up and slapped his daddy with a high-five and celebrated the terrific play. But there was no celebration on the field as the defender lay motionless.

"Dad, why is he not getting up?"

"I don't know, son. He must be hurt."

"But, Daddy, he is not moving at all. Is he dead?"

"No, he's probably being careful not to hurt himself any worse."

"Daddy, I'm scared. That looks bad. Oh God, help him get up!"

They stood there with some forty thousand other spectators that included fans, security, attendants, opponents, coaches, and teammates. But they were no longer watching a football game; the battle now was between one young man and life. Ed didn't really want his son to see this, but what could he do? There was no time to prepare or think of what the fatherly reaction should be. Ed watched as helplessly as his nine-year-old son while treatment was given to the young player on the playing field for the next thirty minutes.

The Rebels pulled out the victory, but it was a quiet trip home for Drew. He thought about the injury much of the way. Upon arriving home, he told his mother all about it. "Mom, there was a player named Chucky Mullins that got hurt bad."

Ed supported his son's account. "It's really serious, Molly; he never moved."

"Mom, do you think he is going to be ok?" Drew asked, becoming emotional once again on this sorrowful day.

"I don't know, honey. I didn't see it. Let's watch the news tonight and see if they can tell us anything."

Their hometown news station, WREG in Memphis, reported that Chucky Mullins had been taken to Baptist Memorial Hospital in Memphis. The initial reports were not good, as they announced that he had not regained movement below his neck.

The news ended and Drew took action. Mental and emotional health professionals tell us that one of the most effective ways to grieve is to perform a constructive task for another. This nine-year-old kid put that principle into practice. He did not fully understand why, but he could not deny the hunger in his soul to *do* something. "Mom, I want to send him a drawing."

"Ok, Drew, we can do that."

Drew broke out his art tools, which consisted of the complete set of Crayola's new state-of-the-art invention, washable markers.

Focused on his work, Drew crafted his most sophisticated version of a stick man playing football. He included words of affection and well wishes. Mom helped Drew put the drawing in an envelope. They found the hospital's address in the yellow pages of the phone book, pasted the 25-cent stamp in the proper location and placed it in the mail box. Molly thought, *at least we can do this much, for this helpless, injured player.* Little did she know that

Drew was just getting started with the process of giving and receiving where Chucky Mullins was concerned. His *impact* upon Drew would last forever.

2: DEFEATED

THE MONDAY FOLLOWING CHUCKY'S INJURY, DREW CONDUCTED HIS normal after-school activities. He came through the front door, dropped his backpack, and headed straight for the fridge. He didn't graze from the ice-box every day, but he usually looked just in case something caught his eye.

Molly met him in the kitchen, and before he opened the door on the shiny white Kenmore he asked the question that was really on his mind. "Mom, have you heard an update on Chucky today?"

"No, honey. They just say that he is still in critical condition."

Drew gazed into the freezer section for a much longer time than was needed to process the frozen offerings. "I'm gonna go draw him another picture."

This practice would continue every day for the next several months. Much like the letters sent to Santa over the years, Molly wasn't sure if they were reaching their destination, but each day Drew would send another drawing across town to Chucky at the Baptist Memorial Hospital.

As the week progressed, it was becoming clear that the injury would create extensive financial hardship for Chucky and his family. The decision had been made by the Ole Miss brass to have a collection for Chucky's medical expenses at the next game. They had set an ambitious goal of raising $50,000 at this one event. Too bad that fate would have it be against LSU—their bitter rival. In recent years, fans of the Red and Blue had not been in a naturally charitable mood following this annual contest. In fact, many felt like the football team was offering enough gratis already by giving most of the games away to LSU. The lowest level staff person at any of the Tunica, Mississippi casinos understands this principle well. Thus, they root hard for the winners and watch their tips pile up on a hot streak. But when the gamblers lose, the spirit of giving flames out just as quickly as it had sparked. Ole Miss had not been on a hot streak in quite some time in this game of skill against the Bayou Bengals.

In 1989, the Ole Miss community possessed a vastly different social culture than that of today. During those days, Ole Miss prided itself on snobbery and for being one of the socially elite universities in the South. Each young man of the student body would wear a navy blazer and his best red tie to home football games. For their part, the female students were clothed in fashionable summer dresses while nothing short of three-inch heels adorned their perfectly manicured toes. Although the navy blazers and summer dresses can still be seen each football weekend, it is no longer a necessity. These days, a fan is just as likely to see students in shorts, wearing baseball caps, or cowboy boots on their feet.

The Ole Miss – LSU rivalry is still intense, but twenty-five years ago it more closely resembled hate. The snobbiest Ole Miss people viewed the typical LSU fan as someone from a totally different country. The more rogue of the Ole Miss followers labeled the bottom of the LSU barrel with the unflattering title of "Coonasses." For the 1989 elitist of the Ole Miss population, a Louisiana Coonass was one step below a "Redneck." They viewed a Redneck as a person lacking appropriate social behavior as a result of their limited cultural exposure or economic challenges. A Coonass, it was believed, was similarly devoid of couth, but their actions were seen to be rooted more in choice rather than circumstances. Most Rebels used a rather simple formula to concoct the social stigmas of 1989. Rednecks couldn't help it, they just were. Coonasses could help it, but liked being rude, loud, and obnoxious. The harshest layer of Ole Miss supporters didn't like the Redneck, but they hated the Coonass.

Ole Miss fans still sing the national anthem before each home game in Oxford. But in those days, regardless of the opponent, the anthem's end would be met with the same battle cry from the entire Ole Miss stadium crowd: "Go To Hell, LSU!"

The Meisenheimers made the road trip to Oxford for the gridiron war with LSU. Ed showed the boys the signs declaring that the University would be collecting donations for the Chucky Mullins' Trust Fund. Molly and Ed had been making an effort to teach young Drew the value of a dollar in recent years. Anytime Drew desired an exorbitant or wasteful purchase, his parents made sure that his allowance fund contributed to some, if not all, of the item. Usually, they had a hearty meal in the Grove before each game, but Drew made a habit of buying his own hotdog inside the stadium. He felt like a big boy making this purchase himself, and as we all know, there is nothing like a ballpark hotdog.

At halftime, there was a moment of silence to honor Chucky and the life-and-death circumstances that had been thrust upon him. When the silence ended, they began passing pails down each aisle of the stadium, seeking donations for his medical expenses. Ed prepared to make a contribution and saw Drew reach for his own wallet. Ed said, "Son, let me put in enough for both of us."

"No, Dad, I really want to give." With that, Drew pulled out the only bill in his little red Ole Miss wallet, a crisp Abe Lincoln. The neighboring fans around them had now begun listening to this exchange—Rebels and Tigers alike.

"Son, that's your whole allowance." It had just dawned on Ed that Drew had not eaten a hotdog at this game.

"I know, Dad, I want to help him get better." One by one, the witnesses to Drew's generosity went back into their wallets. Maybe it was part guilt, or Spirit-led inspiration, but the response was contagious for the fans of both teams. If this kid could give his entire allowance, then they could give a little more.

Ole Miss played with gallant effort, but in the end, effort was not enough, and once again the Tigers were more talented. Drew began to lament on the drive home, "Why can't we be good, Dad? I have been waiting my whole life for us to be *good* and we just keep on being *Ole Miss*."

Ed refrained from pointing out that the woes of Rebel football went beyond the few years of Drew's existence on earth. It was approaching twenty years since Archie Manning had thrilled fans in Oxford and there had been little excitement since. "Son, they played hard today, and we have to be proud of that. Remember, you may not win the game, but you are never a loser if you give your best." Ole Miss fans have been living by statements like this for years, trying to find something to celebrate besides their before-and-after visits to the Grove.

Drew replied, "Kids at my school don't care if Ole Miss played hard. They just laugh at us every time that we lose again."

There was a pause as Ed seemingly had run out of answers. Then he lowered his voice in volume and pitch and slowed his cadence as if he were a natural-born Southerner. "Well, I am proud of one thing today, son. Nobody got hurt like Chucky did last week. Every one of those guys walked off the field today without serious injury."

The statement gave pause to Drew, and he reconsidered. He grew quiet as his dad's words hit home. Drew had been so worried about winning that he had lost sight of the important things in life. Ed sensed his son's reflection and felt he may have placed a little bit of guilt upon Drew. He added, "You know what else makes me proud? That Chucky has friends like you who care enough to help him through this injury."

The morning newspaper shared the results from the fund-raiser.

They had not met the $50,000 goal. Perhaps they had been too bold to have the plea for assistance so soon after the accident. Let's be honest, Chucky was a black kid from Alabama and not a white boy from Jackson, Mississippi. Then of course, LSU could always be blamed for the outcome. No, the giving on this day did not meet the expectations. The actual funds given in just twenty minute's time surpassed $200,000 and far exceeded the most ambitious predictions.

It seems that Drew was not the only one who got a good dose of perspective that day. This was the beginning of the transformation that Chucky Mullins would inspire among all different kinds of people. The University today is made up of a variety of cultures. They are no longer characterized with labels like Redneck or Coonass. Nowadays it doesn't matter so much if people are Red, Yellow, Black, or White. The most important colors today are Red and Blue, and if a person possesses those in their blood then they are part of the same kindred community—the Ole Miss family.

Ole Miss, like people of faith seeking sanctification, is still a work in progress that I don't want to present as being perfect. But Chucky's humble spirit led the way to eroding stigmas that had held for well over a century. Even today, some LSU fans still act like Coonasses, without the Coon. The National Anthem's ending in Oxford is still met by some students of the home team with the indecent cry of: "Go to Hell, LSU!"

But on a monumental day in 1989, some 40,000 enemies joined forces for a common love: football, life, and hope. The Rebels weren't the only ones *defeated* on that day. There was a small victory over race, class, and hate. Perhaps, the truest *defeat* in the 1989 LSU game was to the barriers that separate us from seeing the other as a child of God. *Thank you, Chucky, for bequeathing this gift to our University.*

3: ENCOURAGEMENT

YIPPEE! IT WAS FRIDAY AND CELEBRATION DAY FOR DREW AND school kids everywhere. But there was extra excitement this weekend because it also began a three-week holiday for Christmas break 1989. So Drew stopped by the mailbox on this joyous day with an extra skip in his step. As he peered inside the metal container there was an envelope addressed to "Mr. Drew Meisenheimer" lying on top of the pile. The return address was one that he had grown quite familiar with over the last two months. It was the hospital where Chucky was being treated and the daily recipient of his artwork. He ran inside and yelled, "Mom, I got a letter from the hospital!"

"What hospital sent you mail, honey?"

"Chucky's hospital!"

Afraid this might be some kind of request that Drew stop overloading their mail system with his daily packages, his mom was cautious with her response. "Let me help you open it so you don't cut yourself, Drew." She wanted to give it a look first, in case there was something that might further bruise his fragile emotions where Chucky was concerned.

But Drew was too quick and had it opened before Molly could finish her sentence. She noticed that it was hand-written so she let down her guard a notch and impulsively read aloud.

"Drew, my name is Carver Phillips, and I am the guardian

of Chucky Mullins. You were the first young person to write to Chucky after his injury. Not only that but we were surprised to continue receiving a new letter from you each day. Getting to see your drawings on a daily basis is a highlight of Chucky's day. I would like to invite you and your family to come and meet Chucky in the hospital. Yours truly, Carver Phillips."

"Wow! Mom, he wants to meet me. When can we go?"

"I don't know, honey—let's talk to Dad about it tonight." Any parent knows this is code for: *I don't like the idea, and perhaps I can share the blame of saying 'no' with the other parent.*

Later in the evening, Molly expressed her concerns with Ed that the visit might be too much for young Drew to process. "Ed, we have never seen a paralyzed person lying in a hospital bed. I don't even know how it will affect us, much less Drew."

But Ed felt it could be a healthy experience for their son. "What more can it hurt, Molly? He's already consumed with Chucky and the whole event. Maybe it will help him work through it a bit." Ed ended his argument with an appeal that he knew Molly could not refuse, "Besides that, how can we reject his invitation without being rude?" Ed had played the Southern-hospitality card, and Molly reluctantly agreed. As with most of her decisions, once she was committed, she was all in. She sprang into action, along with Drew and Tyler, making sugar cookies decorated with the number 38 to bring for their visit.

They drove the twenty miles across town to the hospital the first Saturday of Christmas break. Upon arrival, they were surprised to be met by a columnist from a Memphis newspaper, *The Commercial Appeal.* Word had spread about Drew's diligence in writing to Chucky every day and that Drew had given his entire allowance at the LSU game fund-raiser.

Now Molly was really concerned. Remember, this is the same woman that would not throw caution to the wind and let her redheaded Rebel be named Archie. Not only had her son been invited to the hospital room of a quadriplegic, he was now being interviewed for a newspaper story, all within a twenty-four hour period. She wondered what Drew would say as the journalist led him to a seat out of earshot.

The writer began with a softball question, asking what Drew wanted for Christmas, just to get the conversation started. But Drew hit it over the fence with his natural swing in response. "I don't want anything for Christmas this year. I have asked my parents to use my Christmas money to help Chucky get better instead."

The reporter was touched by the sentiment and his instincts told him that this statement wasn't staged by Drew or inspired by his parents. It was the raw emotion of a child discovering the spirit of giving. Drew had been motivated by the magic and joy of living outside of self. He had been pouring his heart into the Chucky Mullins project ever since the accident occurred. Now he was about to meet the fallen soldier for the Red and Blue, and it was time for Drew to receive something in return.

With the newspaper interview completed, the Meisenheimers entered Chucky's hospital room. Drew was composed, displaying a mystifying calm as they walked inside. Chucky could only whisper, but gave a welcoming smile as Drew approached his bed. Chucky showed Drew all of the gifts that he had been given by celebrities and star athletes. Chucky went out of his way to make this little redheaded, buck-toothed, freckled-faced, white kid from Memphis feel comfortable with what he was going through, and he was ok. Chucky must have sensed that Drew was grieving for him, devastated after the tragic event the boy witnessed on a football field. Chucky had seen the countless cards and knew this kid's heart must be broken. So Chucky rallied as he always did, focusing on others rather than on himself. This is the momentous gift that Chucky presented to so many. People would come to him, like the Meisenheimers, seeking to *encourage*, and they would find themselves *encouraged* instead.

Drew responded in a manner that can't be choreographed by parents, or rehearsed by nine-year-old kids. He sat down and scooted the cumbersome wooden chair as close as he could possibly get to Chucky. There was no fear at the sight of the tubes, or the halo bolted to Chucky's head. Drew's next act made his mother lose all the composure she had mustered thus far. He reached over to Chucky and began patting and caressing him. Without words, he offered his affection through this universal sign of love.

Many Christians are aware that a traveling partner of the Apostle Paul was a person whom Paul re-named Barnabas. The meaning for this new name was "Son of Encouragement." Paul knew the importance of having people with spirits of encouragement, like Barnabas, to strengthen him along his journeys. The Bible offers no commentary about how their relationship impacted Barnabas. But I suspect if asked, Barnabas would have said that pouring encouragement into Paul filled his own cup as well. The lines between giver and receiver get blurred when the holy act of encouragement is practiced.

Back in the hospital, it was not clear who was the greater encourager that day: Drew or Chucky. His ever-present smile was there, and Drew had caught the infectious grin. Drew learned a valuable lesson about life that day. He had come to this place in an effort to encourage and give of his cookies. Instead, he found that in the spirit of encouraging, he became the recipient in the process.

Molly, trying to defend herself against the assault on her emotions, looked off to one of the corners of the room. Her eyes rested on the biological children of Karen and Carver Phillips, Chucky's guardians whom she had just met. With her heart already softened by the intensity of the moment, she considered how unwelcoming the atmosphere must be for children. Then she did something very uncharacteristic of her cautious personality. "Karen, can I take Lamar and Keshia home with me for the night? They will have fun with my boys and just be kids for a little while outside of the hospital."

In that moment, two mothers' compassion was joined together. Molly wanted to give, and Karen needed to receive, and in the process they both contributed to the other.

These two mothers were inspired to encourage as they witnessed the examples set by their sons. They had experienced the power of *encouragement* on a level beyond explanation. Molly was not yet aware how much she would need this strength in the days to come. She was about to embark upon her own battle for survival, as she would soon hear she had less than two years to live.

4: HOPE

THE UNIVERSITY OF MISSISSIPPI BEGAN PLAYING FOOTBALL IN 1893 and adopted Yale Blue and Harvard Crimson as their colors. These two Ivy League institutions were the premiere programs during this era of college football and the Rebels had *hopes* of replicating their academic and football success. Three years later the University embraced the nickname Ole Miss. Traditions die hard at the school so the commitment to a tandem representation of both colors and names lives on. On each home game, either red or blue jerseys are worn by the football team and fans are encouraged to dress accordingly.

In 2013, the Princeton Review survey of universities rated Ole Miss as the "Most Beautiful Campus." Many would contend that the prevailing influence was due to the alluring appearance of the female student body. The Oxford campus could serve as a preliminary competition for "Miss Mississippi" at any of the fall football games held there. With each passing year, the current lineage of princesses takes pride in upholding this tradition of beauty. They refuse to be the ones to drop the crown that was passed down by the magnificent matriarchs who came before them. Even more fully than some of the players who will take the field before them, they come with their *game face on.*

Even long-since graduated coeds feel the enticement to still honor this commitment to elegance. Many who grow up in the Baptist faith of the South live by the following mantra: *"Once a*

Baptist, always a Baptist." No matter how progressive their religion may become, they just can't go to church without wearing a dress. It is similarly hard for some alumnae of Ole Miss to relinquish the allure of dressing in their Sunday best, a day early, each fall Saturday in Oxford.

So, it was no surprise when I met Angela in front of legendary coach John Vaught's statue on October 26, 2013, that she was "dressed to the nines." Ole Miss was playing against the University of Idaho, and the athletic department had assigned *blue* as color of the day. Much like when the President of the United States orders the flag to half-staff, it is not a law that one must oblige, but those who do not comply feel unpatriotic. Angela was not about to disrespect the "call-to-color" and was adorned in a stunning blue dress.

But there was one accoutrement to her uniform that was not the norm for fashion-savvy women of Ole Miss. Angela wore a simple white pendant, emblazoned with a red numeral 38. To display such a symbol twenty-four years after Chucky Mullins' injury speaks of tribute in a manner words cannot express.

"I look at his picture each day as I come down the stairs of my home. Just a quick glance is a little reminder for me to *keep on, keepin' on.*" Angela is a nurse practitioner in the field of psychiatry, an area of care where encouragement from an outside source is well served.

The story of Chucky's impact upon Angela begins on that fateful autumn day in 1989 when he was injured. Angela frequented the same social circles as Head Football Coach Billy Brewer and his wife, Kay. When the Vanderbilt game was over, Angela was part of an intimate gathering at the Brewer's home. Billy was quiet and sedate as he waited impatiently for news about his player. This was before the days of everyone having a mobile phone and instant information. He was expecting a call from Head Athletic Trainer Leroy Mullins, who had accompanied Chucky to the Baptist Memorial Hospital in Memphis.

A few hours earlier, the coach had been standing next to Chucky just prior to entering the stadium. The old-school coach rested his hand on Chucky's back—right between the 3 and the 8. Chucky's conscious effort to enter the field with his coach may have been a symbolic statement for the young warrior. *Coach, you gave me a chance, I'm gonna follow you into battle and will not stop fighting for you.* Now the gridiron general was slumped in a chair, in some ways as lifeless as his fallen soldier.

Mrs. Brewer knew that Angela was in the medical field and lived in Memphis. So she asked her to make a phone call to the hospital in an effort to gain some information. When Angela reached someone she knew in the emergency room, the news was not encouraging. She was told that it was an injury to the C4 vertebrae, and he had not regained movement below the neck. Kay called Billy into another room, and Angela broke the news to the coach privately. He was in a state of devastated shock. He expressed a restrained tearful reaction, which few had ever seen. He re-gained his composure and went back into the larger gathering. The night ended with little *hope* for Chucky Mullins' recovery.

Angela worked in the Neurology Department of another medical facility and was not an employee of the Baptist Hospital, so she could not provide any direct care to Chucky or the family. However, she still felt a professional pull to visit the hospital and at least check on him, hoping her clinical training could assist in some way.

She arrived at the hospital on the Monday after the injury and introduced herself to Chucky's guardian, Carver Phillips. He wanted Angela to meet Chucky and welcomed her into his room. Though alert, Chucky was unable to speak and was limited in what he could communicate. Carver escorted her to Chucky's bedside, and Angela was surprised to be met by this smiling young man lying motionless in bed. *This poor fellow has no idea how dark his life is going to become*, she must have reasoned. People trained in psychiatry understand the complexities of the human mind in ways that young twenty year olds suffering from paralysis cannot.

But darkness and depression had no idea what kind of fight it would receive from this beacon of light named Chucky Mullins. "That smile of his could light up the entire world," Angela would later recount.

But early on Angela was not convinced that the smile was real. So she kept coming, waiting for his defenses to drop, searching with all her training for a chink in his armor. She knew that he had to have an emotional crash at some point, and she wanted to be there to help put back the pieces when he did. But with each visit, he continued to express the same balanced emotions. Angela explains, "He was indeed a thermostat person. Too many of us are thermometers and react to whatever is going on around us. But Chucky was a true thermostat. He set the temp in the world around him. He did not let the outside environment impact what he was inside."

So his internal defenses remained true. The injury had paralyzed his body, but would not get his mind. She kept coming, felt drawn to him, and didn't fully understand why. Eventually she would consider that this experience may have benefited her more than Chucky. In this child of God, Angela found *hope*. In the clinical sense *hope* is defined as: *A feeling of expectation and desire for a certain thing to come.* But Chucky would help Angela discover it on a personal level.

"I think that is what it was about Chucky, he gave me *hope*." She, like so many others, was changed by his positive outlook. Her spirits were lifted by witnessing him work through this horrific event with dignity.

"You know *hope* is my favorite word," Angela told me. "That was the name of my precious Yorkie before she died." Sadly, her dog is gone, but on another level *hope* is still there for Angela. She approaches life with the belief that things could be worse, and they will get better. Because of Chucky Mullins' influence, *hope* will never truly die for Angela. So, she looks at his photo every morning and wears her 38 pin every ball game. As stated earlier, traditions die hard at Ole Miss. For Angela, *hope* is one of those traditions that lives on.

Chucky Mullins entering the stadium prior to his injury in the Vanderbilt game, flanked by Coach Billy Brewer and Shawn Cobb (number 44)

5: SMILE

"CLOSE YOUR EYES FOR A FEW MINUTES. IMAGINE THAT YOU ARE lying down completely still. Don't move a muscle. Consider, if you can, that you are frozen in this position. The only part of your body that you have control of is your face. Now you can open your eyes, and the only thing left to do is…smile."

These are the words that Carver Phillips shared with a group of Ole Miss fans on a fall evening in 1989. They had extended Carver an invitation to their meeting, but it was more like a plea. The loyal Rebels supporters sent a driver and an escort, not because he had to go with them, but they needed him to attend the meeting. They were desperate to hear how their beloved injured player was doing. How was he coping with his life that had been forever changed on a football field? Carver and his wife, Karen, were the official parents of record for Chucky Mullins, but now the entire Ole Miss Family was claiming him as their own.

Just a few weeks prior, Chucky had been a vital part of the Ole Miss football team's defense. Now he was lying motionless, exactly like the exercise Carver prompted his audience to experience. But it was not imagination in Chucky's world. For this young Rebel, it was all too real.

So Carver made the trip that evening from the hospital in Memphis, Tennessee to the Ole Miss campus in Oxford, Mississippi, to provide his fans with an update on Chucky's condition. It would be one of Carver's few departures from Chucky's bedside for the duration of his six-month hospital stay.

The heartfelt speech was warmly received as Carver revealed the endearing personality of number 38. "Chucky has high spirits. He's still smiling and laughing like always. While checking on Chucky some people ask how I am doing as well. When I see that *smile* and hear him laugh, every problem, every worry, all the complaining that I used to do, just goes out the door. When I sit there and watch him, and hear no complaints from him about his condition, I realize I don't have a thing to complain about. He just makes me stronger every day."

This, dear soul, is the Chucky Mullins Effect. It was felt by Carver and everyone who ever knew Chucky and called him friend. It has been a quarter century since Chucky's injury but Carver's wife, Karen, remembers as if it were yesterday. "Many days I was down, and I could look at him and think, How can I be down when I look at him? He wouldn't just smile, but he would laugh out loud. We were trying to be positive for him, but he was the one lifting us up."

Chucky had the *smile* long before he attended the University of Mississippi on a football scholarship. I asked his cousin, Dorothy Mullins, to share her fondest memories of Chucky. She told me, "He never had anything bad to say about anyone. Even as a small child he always had a good outlook and attitude. He always had that *smile*."

Critical care hospital rooms deliver an unorthodox impact upon the sensory system of anyone who is unfamiliar with them. The eyes are overwhelmed by everything to look at: wires, tubes, monitors, and constant flow of staff. While the eyes get a workout, the ears are hardly utilized. There is little talking, and other than the constant groaning from a ventilator, or the occasional beep of an instrument, there is minimal noise. The visual imagery of Chucky's room was standard for a victim of paralysis: hospital bed, wires everywhere, tubes in all directions, a halo screwed into his head. But auditory resonation from his room was beyond the norm, there is an unusual sound coming from his new home: laughter.

Chucky lighting up the world with his smile

6: TIME

THE OLE MISS BATTLE CRY FOR THE 1989 FOOTBALL SEASON WAS: *It's Time.* The slogan certainly found its origin in turning around the program. The Rebels had delivered losing seasons the prior two seasons, and the *time* to win was now. But the simple phrase took on multiple meanings to the players. On an individual level, it represented something specific to each person in the locker room. Some saw it as a call to hold nothing back. For the underachiever, it was a reminder to silence the critics around them. For the overlooked players, it was fuel to prove themselves to the naysayers. The occasion had risen for different people all sharing a common call: *It's Time!*

There were several players from the state of Alabama on the team who certainly connected with the war cry. They had developed a kind of "chips-on-their-shoulders" fraternity to prove they could make it in the SEC. They called each other "Bama-Dogs." Chris Mitchell, Louis Gordon, Tony Harris, Deano Orr, and Chucky all lived in rural communities near Florence, Alabama. They would commute to and from Oxford together prior to Chucky's injury. In the summer of 1989, as they crossed the Mississippi-Alabama state line, Chucky began barking like a dog. The others burst out laughing and a new tradition was established. From that day forward, anytime they crossed the state line into Alabama, all five would begin barking like a pack of wild dogs. It was a lively celebration of where they had come from and where they were going.

The Rebels finished the regular season with a record of 7-4. This was a remarkable turnaround amidst the emotional roller coaster surrounding Chucky's injury. The players gathered for a team meeting on the Monday following Thanksgiving, and the spirit was light. The good mood of post-season play was in the air and engulfed the room. The players felt certain that they had been invited to participate in a bowl game but did not know their destination.

Coach Brewer walked into the team meeting and captured the players' attention just seconds after his arrival. After a few introductory details about the bowl selection process, he presented the answer to everyone's question: "Would anybody be interested in playing football in Memphis a month from now?"

The room erupted with energy as each player offered his approval. Sure, the Liberty Bowl was not the most prestigious post season destination. But given a choice this season, Memphis was the perfect setting for the Rebels. That was where their fallen teammate resided, and they were bringing the game to his town. In the cacophony of sound, echoes of "Bama-Dog" and barking rang out in the theater-style room.

The Air Force Academy would be the opponent on December 29. The Academy was favored by more than two touchdowns, and the Rebels were just happy to be playing. During game week, Chucky received daily visits from his teammates and was a part of the boys again. His voice was still weak, not much more than a whisper when he uttered a word. But these visits were not so much about what was said as it was about being together again.

Game day arrived, and the team gathered in the locker room prior to entering the field. The locker room was positioned near an exit tunnel that could support transportation vehicles on and off the playing surface. The distractions of this location could be challenging to a coach preparing a team for battle. But Brewer knew that motivation would not be an issue for his team on this special evening. He had a secret weapon that was about to be unleashed upon this unsuspecting branch of the armed services. Had the entire national defense system of the U. S. Military assisted the Academy, they still would have been over-matched on this night.

As the sound of a vehicle made its way into the tunnel, inside the locker room, Head Coach Dog Brewer tilted his head like a canine for a keener listen. Then he heard it—two short blasts from a siren. That was the signal that he had been waiting to receive. The locker room doors opened and medical personnel filed in, pushing a hospital bed. The secret weapon had arrived. He was wearing a white hat, a red number 38 on his chest, and a big smile across his face.

I remember all of us in the locker room erupting with enthusiasm. My teammates and I had been told earlier in the week that Chucky would not be able to come to the game. It was just too risky to his health to leave the hospital so soon after the injury. Chucky understood the possibility of infection as a result of leaving the hospital, but ultimately the decision was his—there was nothing that could keep him away. We understood his vulnerable situation and knew that Chucky had once more risked his life for our team.

Brewer somehow settled the team down and asked Chucky if he had anything to say. In an instant the room transitioned from an ear-piercing gathering to a spooky-quiet assembly. The Bama-Dog had the floor, and he led the team into battle with the whisper of two words, *"It's Time!"*

If the first outburst had been an explosion, then this was an atomic bomb. The team joined in: "It's Time, It's Time, It's Time!" This sounded more like a celebration than a call to battle. But why would they celebrate? The game had not been played, they were still underdogs, and Chucky was still hurt. He would never walk again…and they were celebrating.

The Rebels went on to win the game by a final score of 42 to 29. Brewer would later recount that his team could have beaten the New York Giants that night.

Sometimes, when we are committed to celebrating, or giving thanks, no matter the outcome, then the outcome is positively impacted by our attitude. In other words, it seems the more thankful we are for what we have, the more we have to be thankful for.

I asked earlier why the team celebrated before the game, as if victory had already been attained. It seems that the entire team took on the spirit of the Bama-Dogs that day. Whenever the five friends crossed the Alabama-Mississippi line there was a celebration. Even though they had not arrived at their destination, they knew that they were on the right road and progress was being made.

If we wait until we arrive to celebrate, then we will miss the wonder along the way. Like the Bama-Dogs crossing the state line together, the team had learned to find joy in both where they had come from and where they were going. When is the last time you celebrated the journey as well as the destination, the effort as well as the outcome? In the spirit of my friend and his Bama-Dogs: IT'S TIME.

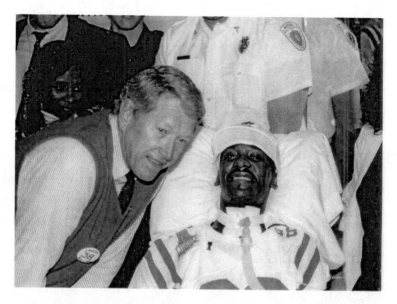

Coach Billy Brewer asking Chucky if he has anything to say to the team

Team responding to Chucky's quote, "It's Time!" pictured clockwise from bottom left: Doug Jacobs, Jody Hill, Marvin Courtney, Scott Swatzell and Ken Williams

7: BLAME

ON DECEMBER 30, 1989, BRAD GAINES AWOKE AFTER AN UNUSUALLY restless night's sleep. It had been two months since Chucky Mullins sustained his injury while tackling the Vanderbilt football star. But it was not the two month anniversary that weighed the heaviest upon Brad Gaines as the date approached. This was the day that he would meet Chucky face-to-face in the Memphis hospital room.

Chucky Mullins came away from their first meeting with four crushed vertebrae, which changed him forever. Brad Gaines also sustained a life-altering fracture on that fateful day. Rather than a horrific obvious injury like Chucky endured, the brokenness that Brad harbored was more deeply felt within himself. The guy who had never known tragedy was feeling his earth shake and was at the breaking point emotionally. He found himself in a bout with depression and the attacking thoughts that he was to *blame* for Chucky's injury. His darkness was so overwhelming that he even felt guilty for feeling so much guilt. *This kid is lying in a hospital bed and can't move, and I am depressed and making it all about me.* It was thoughts like this that Brad was burying deep inside the pit of his soul. *If I had been a little faster or had run the route at a different depth, then Chucky would still be walking and playing.*

So, it was with this heaviness of heart that he went to the hospital to meet his "victim." Growing up as the youngest of four brothers, he had learned the discipline of taking responsibility or accepting *blame* when he had made a mistake. He felt that this visit of paying his respects to Chucky was imperative. If Chucky met him with "coolness" or refused to speak, Brad would understand. He had coached himself to "take it like a man," and absorb whatever punishment the fallen Rebel would dish out. His internal pep talk reasoned with him this way: *Remember, whatever he says to you, you can walk away, but he will still be there.*

When I asked Brad who was present as he was introduced to Chucky, I envisioned an intimate setting. Perhaps the two universities had arranged a private meeting for the players to visit and get through the painful process in a delicate manner. I could also rationalize Karen and Carver Phillips or a couple of Rebel teammates being present for support. But Brad answered my question with this: "It was the day after Ole Miss had won the Liberty Bowl. I was the only outsider there, with about a hundred Ole Miss fans." As a typical SEC football player, he had walked into stadiums with nearly a hundred thousand fans cheering for his demise. But that was nothing compared to the intimidation he felt this day, entering a tranquil hospital room to face the greatest fear of his life.

He had amended his speech throughout the day. But now as the moment of truth approached, he was afraid that none of his words would make a difference. The hulking, 225-pound young man felt as weak and weary as he had ever been. In Brad's mind, *"There were no words, there was no emotion, there were no gifts I could offer Chucky Mullins to replace what I had taken away."*

Countless people had told Brad that he should feel no guilt. But emotions are tricky things. Oftentimes we know what we should believe, but we have no control to put those proper beliefs into gear. Like a love-struck person who has been dumped, they wish they could make the feeling just go away, but the pain remains. Brad did not want to feel guilt or blame, and on an intellectual level knew that he should not, but guilt was still there.

He had heard from professionals, family had reasoned with him, and coaches had pleaded with him. He had been encouraged, and he had been chastised for his guilt, yet none of it affected the guilt that robbed him of joy and peace. None of the words mattered, until he finally heard the most freeing statement that had ever engulfed his ears and soul. Finally, it was not only what was said, but who said it, that made all the difference.

Brad stood by Chucky's bedside, and his mind went completely blank. His prepared remarks left him, and all he could do was look deep within the soulful eyes of the injured one. But without moving a muscle, Chucky Mullins embraced Brad with a bear hug of affection. Chucky, in a coarse and gentle whisper, uttered the most beautiful and resounding message Brad had ever heard, "It's...not...your...fault."

Brad Gaines was not magically cured that day, just as he could not snap his fingers and make Chucky instantly better. Chucky could not do the same for Brad. But healing in our broken world comes in many forms and sometimes takes time. In the following months, Brad made Chucky's life better by becoming another friend to walk with him through his journey. Chucky gave Brad comfort in knowing that he did not hold him to *blame*.

In recent years, Brad Gaines has begun placing less *blame* upon himself for Chucky's injury. This is surely fruit from the emotional and mental maturity which Brad has experienced with the passing of time. It's been twenty-five years since these two warriors of the gridiron first met. Yet to this day, Brad still travels to Chucky's hometown of Russellville, Alabama, three times each year. While there, he tends the grave of the one who lost much but gave much more. Why does he keep going to pay his respect and honor after a quarter of a century? *Blame* it on the offering of love and forgiveness he received from a friend named Chucky.

The hit Chucky made upon Brad Gaines to sustain his injury
(photo © Copyright Bruce Newman, Oxford, MS)

8: VICTORY

IN GREEK MYTHOLOGY, THE WINGED GODDESS PLAYED A PROMI-
nent role in the Titan Wars. According to the ancient fable, she
would majestically soar over the battlefield and bestow accolades upon the victors. The Winged Goddess was named Nike,
which is translated to mean "Victory."

In 1971, an upstart shoe company adopted the name of the
Winged Goddess for its state-of-the art footwear and became Nike,
Inc. The manufacturer created a specially-designed shoe for Michael Jordan to wear in his 1984 NBA rookie season. The sneaker
was released for public sales in 1985 as the *Nike Air Jordan*. These
designer kicks were an instant hit for the shoe company. The *Nike
Air Jordan* flew from store shelves with the same energy as their
namesake—toward a basketball hoop.

By 1989, the *Nike Air Jordan* had transformed from a mere basketball shoe into a popular fashion statement. During this season
in his life, Ed Meisenheimer worked closely with the Nike, Inc.,
distribution center, which was located in Memphis. Ed was fully
aware of the impact Nike had upon the local economy, as well as
its impact on young people throughout the world who idolized the
logo.

Chucky Mullins would be leaving Memphis on February 17th
to receive long-term therapy at Spain Rehabilitation Center in Birmingham, Alabama. The Meisenheimers made arrangements to

deliver a departing gift to Chucky in late January. As they walked into Chucky's room, six-year-old Tyler let the cat out of the bag—or sneakers out of the box—by proclaiming, "We got you some shoes!"

Tyler may have been the whistle on this delivery train, but Drew was the shipping car. He carried the box with as much delicacy as he had done years before as the ring bearer in his aunt Amy's wedding. The gentleness was forgotten as Tyler joined Drew in un-wrapping the package. They tore into the paper with the lightning-quick reflexes of over-sized, air-breathing piranhas. A few seconds into the frenzy it was revealed that Chucky had hit the lottery of footwear and fashion with his very own *Nike Air Jordans*.

At first glance, it appeared the Meisenheimers must have attained an irregular pair of shoes. Ink had recklessly been splattered in a conspicuous manner along the side of the right shoe. The ink was black, fresh, and large, but it wasn't placed there by accident. Not only had the Meisenheimers procured a pair of the hottest-selling shoes on the planet, but they had been personally autographed by the athlete who made them so popular—Michael Jordan. Ed had come through, as he often did, working behind the scenes to transform a good idea into a reality.

As the two families visited and celebrated the gift of the shoes, nine-year-old Drew shared with Chucky his dream of one day being a professional athlete. "I like Michael Jordan, but I want to be a major league baseball player." Drew expressed this desire as if the outcome was foregone.

Drew told Chucky that he had been chosen to play for a travel baseball team named the Central Church Flames. (The term "travel baseball" designates teams that are made up of select players who participate at a higher level of competition than park and recreational teams.) At first, *"Flames"* is a seemingly odd name for a church team. But this is not the first sports team whose mascot is represented by *acts of God,* which the opponent would rather avoid. Who wants to be hit by a *"hurricane,"* washed away by a *"wave,"* or laid out by *"lightning"*? Any good church-goer knows that a chief motivational tool for evangelical Christians includes a warning about the fires found below. So it seems that *"Flames"* is appropriate after all, if you want to scare the blazes out of nine-year-old kids.

Chucky had listened patiently as Drew shared his excitement about the upcoming baseball season. But now as the Meisenheimers were preparing to leave, Chucky had his own comment that applied to baseball and life. "Good luck with baseball—don't ever give up on your dreams. Never quit."

In the weeks ahead it would seem as though Chucky held a prophetic understanding of what was to come for Drew. The adage to *never quit* would keep Drew going through the ups and downs of baseball.

As the season began, Drew quickly found himself at the bottom of the pecking order on his competitive team. He was not prepared for the high level of skill that would be required to receive playing time for the *Flames*. At the depths of his despair Drew would cry out, "I'm not any good! I don't want to play anymore."

This was merely a form of verbal wailing for Drew. He knew quitting was not an option in their family. The household rule was *if you start it, you finish it.* You don't have to play the next season, but you don't quit in mid-stream. Besides that, his hero was Chucky Mullins, and Drew reasoned, *if Chucky's gonna keep fighting, then I am, too.*

Both parents tried lifting Drew's spirits. "Son, it isn't the outcome that matters. There are two things that matter most: attitude and effort."

Drew showed his age by quickly transitioning from wanting to quit, to yearning to play more. "I wish I could be a starter. I never get to play until the game is over. I am tired of practicing. I want to play."

The truth was, Drew had always been an exceptional performer on his recreational teams. He was finding it hard to deal with not being the best player on the field and was reaching out to his parents for comfort.

Ed and Molly had the sixth sense of parental understanding and constantly delivered the verbal medicine Drew needed for his fragile self-image. "It is not how much you get on the field, but how you play the game when you do get to play. The best way to get better and have fun is in practice. Make the best out of that."

Chucky's new home at Spain Rehabilitation Center was cold and drab. It was a white concrete-block room with no view. By March 1990, he had settled into a mundane routine. Each day therapists would work his lifeless limbs, hoping for signs of movement. Like Drew on the practice field, Chucky was seeing no results from all the hard work he had been doing. There were days that Chucky shared Drew's feeling of wanting to quit. No one would have blamed him had he said, *I just want to go home.* But all the while, he *never quit.*

After months of paying his dues on the practice field, Drew finally heard his number called in pre-game stretches. "Number 13, get that arm good and loose. You're starting at second base today."

Drew chose 13 when others said it was bad luck. He intended to change the image for the maligned number, saying, "I am gonna make it a good luck number."

Some people say we create our own luck. Thomas Jefferson described it this way, "I am a great believer in luck, and I find the harder I work, the more I have of it." Drew had worked hard. Lady Luck had played her part, now it was up to number 13 to perform under the big lights.

The hours of therapy turned into days and weeks for Chucky. He kept putting in the work at rehab, like Drew on the practice field. Then one day it happened. One of his arms offered a bit of feeling to Chucky. He reacted to the sensation in a natural manner and attempted to move it. For the first time since his injury, Chucky Mullins maneuvered a part of his body below the neck.

Drew competed relentlessly at practice and eventually got to start in a game. Chucky endured countless hours of therapy and eventually moved his arm. Success often arrives at moments like these, when we least expect it. You work hard for months and see no progress; then out of nowhere the Winged Goddess of *victory* swoops in and crowns you with the victor's wreath.

The Greeks tell us that the Winged Goddess, Nike, did not wait until the war's completion to recognize the accomplishments that propelled *victory*. Instead, she would attend the individual battles to recognize the valor of the brave soldiers. The battlefield was much like the practice field for Drew or rehab sessions for Chucky. That is where we win: practice, rehab...the battlefields of life. May we embrace the fight of Chucky Mullins and Drew Meisenheimer to never quit in whatever conflicts we encounter. You never know when your lucky number will be called or your motionless arm will offer a response.

At first glance, the Nike basketball shoes, given by the Meisenheimers, might appear to be an inappropriate gift for a young man who couldn't walk. But just as Chucky challenged Drew to *never quit*, the shoes served as a form of inspiration to Chucky himself. He intended to one day put them to their proper use, as he walked beyond the battlefield to *victory*.

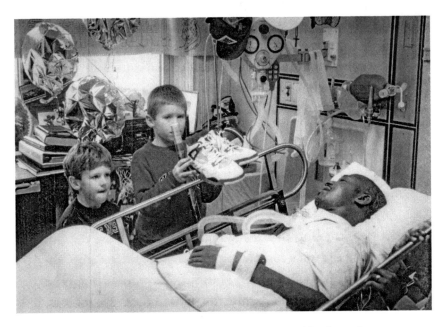

*Drew and Tyler Meisenheimer presenting Chucky with
the autographed Air Jordan shoes*

9: COMPLAINT

IN EARLY MARCH OF 1990, BILLY BREWER TRAVELED TO SPAIN REHAbilitation Center in Birmingham, Alabama. He was anxious to see how Chucky was adjusting to the move to this comprehensive rehabilitation facility. Brewer walked into the therapy room as Chucky was finishing a session. The player was happy to see his coach and greeted him with a smile, saying, "Hey, Coach, give me a few more minutes, and I'll be finished here. Then we can go to my room." It was difficult for the coach to watch Chucky's lifeless limbs being moved by others. He saw puffy flesh in the shell of a body that just months prior had housed a mass of sculptured muscle. By the time therapy was finished, Brewer's heart was heavy as he considered the plight of his young player.

Once they arrived at Chucky's personal space in the facility, Brewer's mood quickly transitioned from sorrow to anger. With his emotions already heightened, it did not take a lot to bristle the hair on the back of Dog Brewer. Immediately after entering the room he stepped back outside and said to a nurse, "Where is your supervisor? I need to issue a *complaint*."

As he waited for the supervisor at Spain Rehabilitation Center, his mind drifted back to three months prior. Coach Brewer was sitting in his office early one morning and received a prank call.

"Hello, is this Coach Billy Brewer?" the caller asked.

Brewer used these early morning hours in the office as private time to prepare for the day. He was less than excited about the interruption and offered only a few curt words to convey his annoyance. "Yes, it is."

"Good Morning, Coach Brewer. Would you please hold for the President?"

The prankster had not done his homework regarding the executive structure of the University and Brewer was happy to call his bluff: "You need to check your facts a little better. We don't have a President here at the University. We have a Chancellor."

The caller stepped it up a notch and did not relent, "Sorry for the confusion, sir. Will you hold for the President of the United States, George Bush?"

Thoroughly amused now, Brewer played along. "Why sure, I would love to talk to ol' Georgie. Put him on!"

After a few moments, the silence on the line was replaced by a familiar-sounding voice. "Hi, Coach Brewer. This is George Bush. Thank you for taking my call."

In a flash Brewer thought, *if this is a prank then it's a darn good one because he sounds exactly like the President of the United States.*

"Coach, I was sorry to hear about your injured player, Chucky Mullins. I wanted to give you a call and offer my condolences to Chucky and the team."

Brewer, finally convinced that he truly was talking to President George Bush, shared some intimate remarks about Chucky. "Mr. President, let me tell you a little bit about the character of this young man. From the moment Chucky Mullins walked onto the Ole Miss campus, he never asked me for anything. Most players always have at least one problem that I need to deal with. They either get in trouble or have specific needs that require my involvement. Chucky never asked for one single thing and never caused one ounce of trouble."

Brewer had grown accustomed to kids from one-parent or fos-
ter-parent homes finding it difficult to adjust to the discipline required
for college football and life. It was not that Brewer did not sympathize
with his players in need. He just could not understand how Chucky
did not display the requests typical of his challenging background.

President Bush was moved by what he heard and offered an
invitation to Brewer. "Coach, I am scheduled to be in Memphis
this week, and I would be honored if you would meet me at the
hospital to visit with Chucky." They worked out the details of their
meeting that morning. It was indeed not a prank; Chucky would
be receiving a visit from the President of the United States.

Brewer arrived at Chucky's room early on the day of the scheduled Presidential visit. He eagerly shared the good news, "Chucky,
you're gonna have a special visitor today."

"That's good, Coach. Who is it?"

Brewer, not wanting to spoil the surprise, kept his player guess-
ing. "Well, you're the nickel back on our team. So we wanted you
to meet the really Big Nickel." The sun was shining brightly into
Chucky's room that day in Memphis. Chucky glanced at the pleth-
ora of professional sports memorabilia on display and wondered if
it was one of his prior benefactors.

Now, three months after the Presidential visit Brewer sat with
Chucky in his new room at Spain Rehabilitation Center.
Brewer knew how much President Bush's visit had inspired
Chucky. But as he looked around Chucky's room he saw a
dreary setting. None of the keepsakes that had adorned his
room in Memphis were there, and Chucky had no view of
the outdoors. Brewer was concerned that this dismal setting
would have the opposite effect of the Presidential visit.

When the medical supervisor arrived, Brewer cornered him
outside the room for a private consultation. "Hello, sir. I would

like to speak with you about getting this young man moved to another location in your facility. This room is so cold-looking it even makes me depressed. You gotta give him a little more hope here. He was looking face-to-face with the President of the United States recently, now he can't even look outside. He doesn't have a view at all! Let him see a bird, a tree—some signs of life beyond this room."

The legendary SEC coach was frustrated that he could not *make it all better* for his player. So he focused his efforts on what he could change. That is the nature of Billy Brewer—he is a fixer, one who works to repair people and circumstances. In short, Brewer was doing what he always did, fighting for one of his players, giving him a chance to succeed. Chucky's room was reassigned before Brewer left the facility that day.

Today, Brewer remains enamored by Chucky's approach to life and football. "I never heard him offer a single *complaint* before or after the injury. Players would come to me at times with the *complaint* that they needed more playing time. That was not Chucky's way of responding to a problem. He paid his dues on the scout team and worked hard at everything we asked him to do."

It seems that Chucky was not a person of *complaint* because he embodied a spirit of contentment. He had an innate passion to be happy regardless of the situation in which he found himself. This is not to say that Chucky was complacent. There are subtle but monumental differences in how Chucky embraced contentment rather than complacency.

It was because Chucky was not complacent that he made his journey through Spain Rehabilitation Center and not simply home to Russellville. However, it was because he was a person of contentment that he offered no *complaint* about his accommodations. He was content with what he had, but he was not complacent in what he could become.

Chucky Mullins was a person for whom people like Billy Brewer were willing to fight. I suspect if Brewer was asked to wage another battle for Chucky Mullins today, his response might be, *I would have no complaint.*

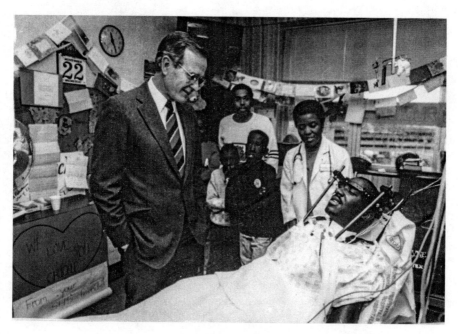

President George H.W. Bush visiting Chucky in Memphis

10: GONE

TWO DAYS AFTER CHUCKY MULLINS MOVED FROM MEMPHIS TO BIR-
mingham, the Meisenheimers would embark upon a journey of
their own. It was a pilgrimage on which they had never *gone*, and it
would take them miles away from the stable world they had known.

On Monday, February 19, 1990, Molly was in the shower getting a jump-start to her day. This was one of the few places the
thirty-five-year-old mother could have some privacy. But her solace
was abruptly invaded by an intruder. The assaulter had not entered
the room, but her body. Molly felt something in her breast that
was foreign to her touch. It seemed small and innocuous but would
prove to be the largest obstacle she ever faced. She thought to herself, *Is this what they call a "lump"?*

Molly's question would be answered with a biopsy on Friday,
March 9, 1990. She had breast cancer.

The following Monday, Molly had her first appointment with a
surgeon. From the outset, Molly asked the man in the lab coat to
shoot straight with her and not sugar-coat her condition. At times
his aim was a little too much on target, as his hard facts pierced
the bull's eye of her heart. In the days ahead, the family would
affectionately refer to him as Dr. Gruff in reference to his abrasive
bedside manner.

The seasoned physician embraced Molly's appeal for frank-
ness with enthusiasm, as he delivered the treatment plan with the

smoothness of a porcupine. "You need to have mastectomy surgery immediately."

Molly started rambling, as much to herself as the physician. "I will need a couple of days to prepare before the surgery. Drew has baseball practice tomorrow. We are out of milk, and I usually go to the store on Mondays..."

Dr. Gruff interrupted her in mid-sentence, "Molly, your life, as you know it, has changed. You need to get your affairs in order. If this cancer has spread to other parts of your body...then two years from now you could be *gone*."

Molly took a deep breath and responded in a more paced and softer tone. "Doctor, I appreciate your honesty, which is what we asked of you. But I need a couple of days to get myself mentally prepared. Tomorrow, I will take care of these important events in the life of our family. I will go to the store and attend Drew's baseball practice. I will be ready to have the surgery on Wednesday." Molly was not asking for permission from the physician. She explained, beyond doubt, how these events were going to transpire.

> Just because we have received life-and-death news, we don't stop doing the little things that make us family. Instead, we interact with more appreciation and respect for the gift of time that we have together.

Sure, Dr. Gruff understood the complexities of cancer and surgery. But Molly knew instinctively how to best nurture her family through this darkness. Life doesn't stop for cancer and neither did Molly. This is how she intended *"to get her affairs in order."*

Molly's condition would deteriorate quickly over the next few months. Many days, she merely existed. Through it all, the family would continue to function as normally as possible. Ed kept working to provide for the family, Tyler participated in summer escapades with the neighborhood kids, and Drew was in full swing with the *Flames* baseball team.

There were days that Molly wanted to quit treatment. The pain was agonizing. She and Ed decided to fight the cancer as aggressively as possible, and she was feeling defeated from the pounding the chemo was giving to her body. (These days, medical professionals do not offer the extreme treatment of combining the following four medications that Molly agreed to: Cyclophosphamide, Doxorubicin, Oxaliplatin, and Methotrexate).

Chucky Mullins had moved to Birmingham but was not forgotten by Drew. He may have been *gone* from Memphis, but his presence still hovered at the Meisenheimer home. "Mom, you can get better, like Chucky is getting better." Chucky, by way of Drew, had become a great source of strength and encouragement for Molly. Chucky was giving hope to Drew, which indirectly helped Molly and gave her peace as a mother. It was comforting to know that her child could focus upon her illness with a brighter outlook.

On June 20, 1990, Molly mustered her strength to attend her first and last *Flames* game of the season. She donned a baseball cap of her own to camouflage the lack of hair on her head. Cancer had attacked her body, and it was winning. But Molly rallied for this one game, exhausted and hurting. She knew that Drew was no longer the best player on the field, so Molly was in attendance to watch her favorite player sit on the bench.

Drew looked into the stands from his familiar perch on the bench and was shocked to see his mom there. Molly had kept her appearance a secret from her oldest son so she could surprise him. Her presence at the game was a celebration of her inspirations: Chucky and Drew. They were still fighting and so was she.

The coach of the Flames was a fiery character that we will call Coach Sparks. He was a wild man on the diamond and took winning seriously. But the competitive coach must have had a soft side as well. He had heard that Molly would be a spectator on this day—and put Drew in the starting lineup.

Drew approached the on deck circle for his initial at bat with a bit of shake in his step. This was a life-giving moment for Molly, getting to see her son play. Regardless of the outcome, he knew she was there and the effort it had taken.

Drew entered the batter's box for the first time and gave his mom a big wave. The first pitch was right down the middle of the plate. Drew swung for the fence and surpassed his mark. The ball did not stop traveling until it was beyond the grasp of the nearest fielder, safely on the other side of the outfield fence. Molly yelled out in her weakened voice, "It's GONE!"

Molly only attended one game the entire season, and she witnessed Drew's first official homerun. She had certainly *gotten her affairs in order.*

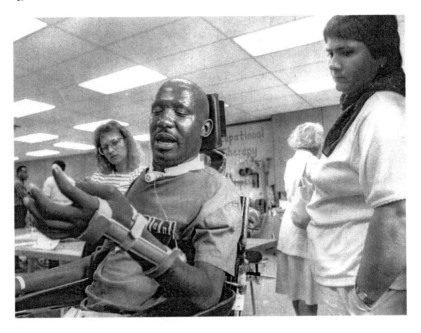

Chucky in therapy at Spain Rehabilitation

11: COVERAGE

IT WAS A SPIRIT-FILLED DAY OF WORSHIP AT THE WALNUT GROVE Missionary Baptist Church in Jackson, Tennessee. An old familiar song played during the call for altar prayer, and one of the congregants felt the inspiration to respond. As the gentle giant walked down the aisle of the house of worship, he could feel the presence of the Holy Spirit, as if they were holding hands.

The choir was singing *Come Ye Disconsolate* and the lyrics engulfed the soul of the young man. He made it to the altar, closing his eyes as these words clothed his fragile emotions: *Earth has no sorrow that heaven cannot bear.* He wiped away the well of tears that were now running down his cheeks.

He had staked his faith in Jesus Christ years before in this very spot. So this meeting at the altar was not a beginning to his journey. Instead, it was a celebration of the One who had walked with him every step along the way.

The pastor knew the twenty-one-year-old man well. His ancestors had been a part of the worship community since the church's inception in 1883. The minister began to speak in the pulpit, but the pastor's words were lost in the troubled mind of his weary parishioner. The journeyman had knelt in prayer and was uttering over and over, "But for the grace of God there lay I."

The cleric felt that the young disciple was having a deeply spiritual experience, reflecting on how God's grace had saved him from his sin. But the young man was pondering the real-life tragedy that had occurred on a football field.

"It could have been me…" he finally added as he raised his gaze toward the heavens.

Weeks before, a photo had circulated of Shawn Cobb with Chucky Mullins and Coach Billy Brewer. It would become the iconic photo that was taken just prior to Chucky's last game. But on this day, in the house of God, Shawn no longer had the strength to stand. He made his way back to the pew, and in some ways, felt the brokenness of his injured teammate.

"It could be me with a broken neck, if not for the grace of God." He had finally said what was truly on his heart. It was spoken as a prayer of thanksgiving for his health and grief for a friend's injury.

But there was a deeper pain that Cobb could not bring himself to utter that day. Chucky's tackle was against the receiver that Cobb should have had in *coverage*.

Over time, Cobb drew the strength to explain the events as if he were a play-by-play announcer. "We were in man *coverage*, and I was supposed to pick up the back if he released from behind the line. I didn't get to him in time, but Chucky did. It still crosses my mind at times. What if I had been there to cover Brad Gaines? Would Chucky have made the hit?"

Chucky's last play was eerily similar to his first big play as a Rebel. Ole Miss was playing Georgia, and the Bulldogs had the ball in the Rebels' red zone (red zone denotes the area of the field inside the twenty-yard line). Chucky Mullins was inserted as the fifth defensive back in the Rebels' nickel package. On cue, a pass was thrown, and Chucky made a spectacular defensive play. He leaped up at the last second and batted down the pass just as it was approaching the receiver's hands. It was a touchdown-saving play.

The play evolved because the receiver out of the backfield had become open. The linebacker, Cobb, was coached to stay in front of the back with his hands up. The back broke further downfield and gained some separation. Shawn had not made a mental mistake or blown the *coverage*. He was a brilliant student of the classroom and the game and was rarely out of position. He was the middle linebacker, the enforcer of the defense. His job was first and foremost to stop the run. Any help he could provide covering receivers was secondary to his primary responsibility. The Georgia running back was preparing to grasp the well-thrown ball when Number 38 came to the rescue and batted it away. The pass fell, incomplete, and the field sign changed to read *4th down*.

Cobb was well aware that Chucky had picked up his slack and made mention of it when they got to the sideline. "Hey, 38! Thanks for covering my hind end out there." Shawn Cobb was, and is, a true gentleman of class and faith. "Hind end" was the crudest language he could bring himself to say, even in the heat of battle.

Chucky's response showed his natural leadership in lifting up others, "Hey, Bro, I got yo' back! I should have intercepted it, though." Rather than let Cobb dwell on his failure, Chucky shared his own shortcoming. That is what teammates do. One goes down, another steps up and picks up the *coverage* for his fallen brother. Together, Shawn and Chucky transformed the problem into an opportunity for 38 to shine.

After the 1989 fall semester ended, Shawn returned home and worshiped every week at the Walnut Grove Missionary Baptist Church. Less than a year after the injury, Chucky made his own return trip home. His home was no longer Russellville but now Oxford. Despite being a quadriplegic, he was returning to campus to continue his education.

Shawn was present in the crowd for Chucky's return to Oxford on that August day in 1990. Cobb was joined by all of his teammates, coaches, the Ole Miss band, and what appeared to be half of the Ole Miss student body and faculty. It was on this day that Cobb heard the words spoken that gave meaning to Chucky's injury and more substance to Cobb's own life. It would take Cobb several years to put it all together. But the puzzle pieces for finding peace with this tragedy were taken out of the box for Cobb on that faithful summer day.

Shawn would later explain, "I will never forget Chucky speaking to the large crowd of people when he returned to Oxford." Shawn paused, remembering how this event had been burned into his memory. "Chucky told us, 'I am thankful to all of you for coming here today. Always thank the Lord and never quit.'"

In 1998, Shawn and the love of his life, Tammy, joined together in the union of holy matrimony. Today, their family is complete with three beautiful daughters, Jamisen, Jadyn, and Jordyn. The lone man of the household said, "We have a family motto: Cobbs never quit." The motto is a tribute to his friend and teammate, Chucky Mullins, who first uttered these words in August of 1990.

I asked Cobb why he thought Chucky was able to respond so well to adversity and bring inspiration to innumerable people. He offered the following poetic response:

"In essence, Chucky's story is the ultimate American dream. He started with little and heard people doubt his ability to succeed. Despite encountering many obstacles, he refused to give up. He worked hard for everything. Then, in the face of tragedy, this young man said, 'I will always thank God, and I will never quit.' There is no better inspirational story than that of Chucky Mullins."

"Why was Chucky able to respond to adversity so well? I still don't know. Only God knows," Shawn says. "Chucky just happened to be called off the bench to go play for a while. He made a big play and a bigger impact upon so many people. And then God took him out the game and sent him back home."

In addition to the Cobb family's commitment to each other, *Cobbs never quit*, Shawn has also not forgotten Chucky's commission to always thank God. To this day, when Cobb returns to his home church for worship, he remembers the first time he went to the altar after Chucky's injury. He always offers prayers of thanksgiving in this sacred place. And sometimes while sitting in the house of worship, he utters the words that Chucky first said to him on the football field, "Hey, Bro, I got yo' back!"

Shawn Cobb is still a giant among men. Nowadays not so much for his physical appearance but because of the man, husband, and father he has become. He attributes a portion of his development to a teammate from long ago. "Chucky's inspirational story continues, to this day, to have influence upon my life." Chucky gave *coverage* to Cobb in the Georgia and Vandy games, and now Cobb covers Chucky's back by living in his spirit on a daily basis.

As said earlier, that is what teammates do—one goes down, another steps up and picks up the *coverage* for his fallen brother. Together, Shawn and Chucky transformed the problem into an opportunity for 38 to shine.

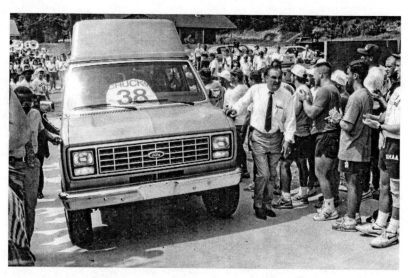

Chucky's arrival at his new home in Oxford

12: CREEK

IT'S SEPTEMBER 22, 1990, AND OLE MISS IS PLAYING ARKANSAS, IN LIT-tle Rock. The Rebels have the lead 21-17 with a few seconds remaining in the game. But the Razorbacks have the ball on the five-yard line and time for one more play. The ball is snapped and running back Ron Dickerson receives it on an option play. He runs to the left and shakes off the hit from a defender at the three-yard line. He lunges for the open space between him and the goal line for the game-winning score. Out of nowhere, he's hit one foot from the goal line by a human wrecking ball in white. Time runs out as the Razorback is taken down by Number 38 of the Rebels, preserving the win.

It was the most amazing play that I had ever witnessed while participating in a football game. I was in a state of joyful shock as I watched from the sidelines. With no timeouts remaining, the last few seconds slipped off the clock with Arkansas helpless to stop it. I ran onto the field, celebrating with my teammates. I was overcome with emotion. This moment would become known in the history of Ole Miss football simply as "The Hit."

The heroic effort of Number 38 on this fall day was set in motion several months prior. Chris Mitchell was exiting the weight room as Coach Billy Brewer was entering. "Hey, Big Man, let me talk to you a minute," Brewer said while grasping the arm of his senior defensive back. The grip on Mitchell's upper limb was more of a caressing tug than an assault upon his personal space. With this gesture, Brewer communicated even more about this impromptu meeting. What he had to say was important, but it would be a warm conversation. Brewer was skilled at asserting himself with body language and facial expressions that surpassed words.

"Yes, sir, Coach, what's up?" Mitchell responded with the level of respect that he gave to all of the staff—not just the Big Dog.

"What do you think about wearing Number 38 this year?" Brewer didn't have to say why he would be wearing it; Mitchell understood the significance.

"Yes, sir, that would be good, that'll be real good."

Chris Mitchell was the natural choice to honor Chucky Mullins by wearing his jersey number. He was born in Town Creek, Alabama, just thirty miles from Chucky's home of Russellville. They quickly became friends at Ole Miss, and Mitchell gave Chucky the nickname "Hagler" because he had the looks and fighting spirit of professional boxer Marvin Hagler. Chucky joined with other teammates in calling Mitchell "Creek," in reference to his hometown. Besides Mitchell's personal connection with Chucky, he was what legendary Florida State coach Bobby Bowden would have called a "dad-gum" good football player. Creek was an exceptional leader, gave maximum effort, and had a winning attitude. These were qualities that Brewer highly valued, and they personified the spirit of what would become known as *The Chucky Mullins' Courage Award*.

The first game of the season was against Memphis State in Oxford. In his debut wearing number 38, Creek Mitchell sealed the victory by intercepting a pass late in the game. Chucky watched every play from his perch on the front row in the stands. He was positioned on the twenty-yard line, right behind his teammates' bench. When the game was over, Creek came over to Chucky and asked, "How'd I do?"

Chucky's masterful response relayed his sense of humor and affection for his teammate. "You did pretty good, but I saw you miss a few plays." Everyone laughed. Chucky was relentless at making light of his circumstances and creating laughter whenever the opportunity arose. Creek had come seeking approval and Chucky busted his chops. This is how friends interact—regardless of their physical state. It was Chucky's way of communicating to all those around him: *Don't feel sorry for me, I'm enjoying my life, now you live yours to the fullest.*

The Rebels lost against Auburn the next week in Jackson. Creek Mitchell became extremely focused after the loss. Chucky had meant his words as a joke to Creek, but they stung a bit. Mitchell asked himself, *Did I give every ounce of myself in the first two games? Did I take any energy off the field that could have been spent?* In Chucky's words, *'Did I miss any plays?'* Creek was visiting with Chucky a few days before the Arkansas game and pouring his heart out. "Dog, we not gon' lose to Arkansas. I'm not starting this season 1-2. We gotta bring it Saturday." Chucky wisely gave no instruction but just listened to his friend as he worked out his problem.

When I asked Creek about The Hit that ended the Arkansas game, he gave me an un-boastful but accurate response. "Man, Jody, people ask me a lot about The Hit. Truth is, I don't remember much about it. I made 21 tackles that day, and some of those were a lot harder hits than the last one." For Creek to tally 21 tackles as a defensive back is mind-blowing. To record such a high number of hits would be phenomenal for any defender on the field. But it was other-worldly for him to make that many put-outs from his safety position. Consider as well that the safety is the last line of defense and begins each play furthest from the ball. This distance allowed him to be running top speed before each collision. Much like an automobile crash, the velocity of the moving objects increases the damage upon impact. Yet after each wreck, Creek willingly climbed back into the car—21 times that day—embracing each meeting with full force and energy. Besides the numerous tackles, there was another reason why Creek did not remember much about the details of The Hit. He downplayed a possible concussion saying, "I jammed my neck a little bit on that last play." Sustaining pain and dizziness, he had left it all on the field.

Creek would go on to produce multiple game-saving plays for the Rebels that year. He was named to the All-SEC team and led his squad emotionally and physically to a 9-3 record. The Rebels were rewarded for the successful season by receiving an invitation to play in their first New Year's Day bowl game in twenty years. Two years after his exceptional season, Creek Mitchell was chosen as one of 27 players for the Ole Miss Football Team of the Century.

I wonder if Creek Mitchell would have accomplished all those accolades had he not worn 38 that year. I am not suggesting that he received preferential treatment—or sentimental votes—because he was honoring Chucky. He certainly deserved the recognition, regardless of what number he was wearing. The meatier question may be this: Would he have played that hard had he only been playing for himself?

Chris Mitchell's hometown of Town Creek, Alabama, resides only a few miles from the Tennessee River. To look upon this massive body of water is awe-inspiring. The great river is used to produce electrical power, with the help of the numerous generators constructed within its massive banks. But the Tennessee River would not be so glorious without the countless tributary rivers, creeks, and channels that feed into it. These lesser bodies give all of themselves to become part of something larger. The river needs the creek, and the creek becomes the river.

The more I understand Creek Mitchell, the more I see his

nickname as a fitting tribute to the inspiration he received from Chucky. Like the waters near his hometown, Creek took on the number 38, and gave all he had for something that was bigger than himself. I believe he found a power and strength that he would have never realized in his own existence. As a small stream pours every drop into a larger flow, he emptied himself into being number 38 and became something more. Chucky called him CREEK, and he called Chucky HAGLER. They joined forces to become a river of courage that continues to flow throughout the South.

Chucky and Chris "Creek" Mitchell

13: DEDICATION

WHEN CHUCKY RETURNED TO OXFORD IN THE SUMMER OF 1990 to resume his education, his guardian, Carver Phillips, was with him. Carver had remained by Chucky's side throughout the ten-month transition to his new life after the injury. Carver's wife, Karen, preceded Chucky and Carver's arrival in Oxford by a month. She, along with the help of her two young children, Keshia and Lamar, would ready their new house for Chucky's arrival.

Karen could count on one hand the number of times she had been to Mississippi, and now this was her new home. "I didn't know anybody there, and it was quite an adjustment from my hometown of Russellville." Still, she had lots of visitors who eased the transition. "I will never forget the daily visits I received from Chucky's teammates: Bill Bush, Snake Williams, Louis Gordon, and Chris Mitchell were always there."

Later, when Chucky would spend time with these friends, he would call it, "Jawing with my boys."

He may have called them *boys,* but in Karen Phillips' eyes they were responsible young *men.* "They were in college and could have been out chasing girls and going to parties but they went out of their way to come see Chucky and our family."

When I asked these guys what stirred this *dedication* to Chucky, they offered a variety of answers. But the motivating factor for each was centered between two themes that I will attempt to describe in this chapter.

Although Chris "Creek" Mitchell was the first person to wear the number 38 in honor of Chucky, it was not the first time he had experienced the tragic injury of a loved one. In his senior year of high school, Chris was practicing basketball when he heard a yell across the gym, "Chris, there's been an accident!" Only a few seconds would pass before his questions would be answered, yet his mind raced in the typical manner: *what kind of accident, who was it, how bad are they?* The answer came, "Your brother was walking across Highway 72 and was hit by a car. He's in critical condition."

This shocking news was reminiscent of another horrific accident that had occurred two years prior when six people had been hit in almost exactly the same location by an eighteen-wheeler. Two of them died and the other four were hospitalized for an extended time. One of the injured was a seven year old little girl who was a youth cheerleader for the Hazelwood High Golden Bears. She would join Mitchell, his teammates, and the high school cheerleaders on the sidelines each week before the injury. The accident put the little angel in a body cast for nearly a year, and Chris felt compelled to reach out to her. "I visited her almost every day in the hospital because she was part of the team." Now this dangerous piece of black-top had claimed another victim. This time, as his brother held on between life and death, it was even more personal.

Chris did what came naturally to him in response to his brother's injury. Although his younger sibling would remain in the hospital for over a month, Chris went to see him—every single day. When Chris told me about visiting with his brother, he did not offer an explanation, as he had for the young girl. He presented this behavior with the understanding that his actions needed no explanation. I suspect he must have reasoned: When family is hurt, or in need, you go to them.

It was Chris' experience that prompted him to respond to Chucky's injury with similar *dedication*. After each game during his senior season at Ole Miss, he would travel to the Phillip's home to hang out with Chucky. If it was a road game and the team got home late, he went. If he had been injured and felt like just going to bed, he went. After he made game-winning plays for the Rebels and everyone wanted a piece of his time and popularity, he went.

Even beyond his playing on the field, Chris represented the character of Number 38. Coaches will often say it's the preparation that a team makes when no one is watching that makes the difference on game day. Though the crowds were gone, the cameras packed away, and the click of typewriters had been silenced, Chris concluded each fall Saturday with the same faithful visit. No one would be watching, but the two 38's just wanted to be together.

Chris told me the story of his brother and the young cheerleader to help me understand his *dedication* to Chucky. He closed with these words, "Chucky is my teammate and the youngest of the Bama-Dogs! He will always be my younger brother!" For Chris, he visited the young cheerleader because she was a teammate. He was committed to his brother because he was family. He spent time with Chucky because he was both.

Karen remembered four friends for their exceptional care to Chucky. "They went out of their way to do random acts of kindness for our family. Each time Louis Gordon would fill up his car with gas at the Wild Bill's convenience store he would bring us some of their delicious catfish nuggets."

The foursome described their reasoning for the daily stopovers with words like: "Friend, buddy, partner, and home-boy." But I believe Chris Mitchell spoke for them all when he described Chucky with these two powerful nouns: teammate and brother.

Friends like Snake, Louis, Bill, and Chris made sure that Chucky's emotional tank was always full. It was *dedication* like this that gave Chucky the fuel to move the world from his motionless state.

Chucky with teammates
from left: Trea Southerland, Louis Gordon and Maurice Shaw

14: RECEIVER

MY SON, NOAH, BEGAN HIS FOOTBALL CAREER AS A 7TH GRADER playing for his middle school team. For better or worse, he had not participated in park league ball for several years like some of his friends. As parents, we were hopeful that he would get a little playing time and stay healthy on his maiden outing.

My wife, Monya, and I were anxious parents as his first game of the season approached. We had been rehearsing pep talks for after the game, in case he did not get to play. To our surprise, he got on the playing field early in his initial contest. In fact, he actually took the majority of game-snaps at wide receiver. His mom and I were ecstatic to visit with him after the game and congratulate his accomplishment. He came into our presence and said with dismay, "I didn't get to touch the ball!"

I reminded him that there were several skilled players on his team and laughingly responded, "Dude, you are lucky that you touched the field, you will get to touch the ball eventually."

Many of us embrace Noah's desire to "touch the ball" as we participate in the game of life. We don't want to sit on the sidelines and simply watch. We want to live, play, or work at the highest level possible. It is more appealing to be the quarterback of your life rather than the *receiver* of whatever the world throws your way.

Chucky Mullins possessed this hunger to participate at the highest level in life, as on the field. Although he played defensive back in college football, Chucky was a natural-born passer who distributed the ball in his relationships. Like any good signal-caller, he deflected recognition and offered praise to others.

Jeff Carter was a teammate who became the second player to wear the number 38 jersey in Chucky's honor. "As freshmen, we were on the scout team together and that is not always a fun place to be," Carter said. The scout team is often made up of young players who practice against the starters. They do their best job to imitate the next week's opponent in practice. The practice squad is sorely overmatched in skill and it can be a demoralizing experience. Carter, recounting their scout team brotherhood, said, "Chucky had a way of making it fun and keeping you up." He fondly remembers Chucky joking and making his friends laugh. "When he was no longer with us in the meeting room and at practice I missed him terribly. I yearned for the little things he would do to make everybody's day better—those random acts that you don't notice so much until they're not there." Chucky, like any good field-general, made those around him better.

In an instant after the injury, Chucky's life drastically changed. He had been a giver to others and then he had to become a *receiver*. Imagine the emotional roller coaster this must have been for Chucky. He had been the one giving, an extrovert, always with the guys. Now he was receiving, no way to reach out, and often alone with his thoughts.

How do you cope and keep going when so much of what you have loved is taken away from you?

Chucky somehow transitioned into his new position off the field with flawless skill. The manner in which he contributed to the world had been taken away, but his desire to contribute had not. His first method of becoming an accomplished *receiver* was by allowing Carver to read the Bible to him. Carver was doing one of the few things he could in the early stages of the injury and Chucky did not rebuff his efforts. He could have refused to listen, not accept this form of care from Carver. But Chucky accepted it gracefully, just as Chucky had so readily offered in times past. This was his way of giving now, by *receiving* from another, and allowing them the joy of giving to him.

After Chucky returned to Oxford to continue his coursework, the entire Phillips family joined in to assist with the exceptional needs he had on a daily basis. The simple task of getting dressed is something that the average person doesn't consider. But this was a cumbersome ordeal for Chucky that required the assistance of others.

He trusted only Karen to choose his clothing each day. The nurses and paid caregivers could not perform this task to his liking. Karen beams with a big smile when she remembers, "He would tell them, 'Go get Karen to pick out my clothes—she knows what I like.'" She was also the only person who Chucky thought could handle the delicate assignment of selecting his music. Not just anyone could turn the dial to the exact right number. Even more complex was setting the proper volume. Doesn't sound so hard, right? It seems anyone could have performed these mundane tasks, had Chucky not been the recipient. But Chucky understood that the best way he could love Carver and Karen in his immovable state was to accept love from them. He allowed them to "do for him" and continued to love by being a *receiver*.

I shared earlier my son's frustration after his first football game as a *receiver*. Noah did eventually touch the ball as an eager seventh grader. He ran a simple five-yard-out pattern and the quarterback sailed the ball his way. He caught it just as the defender made contact and wrestled him to the ground. There isn't a lot of smiling in football, but we could see Noah's face light up from our perch in the stands. As his parents, we could not have been any happier if he had just set a new record for the most receptions in the NFL.

To the casual observer, there was nothing exceptional about the play. As in so many situations, one has to know the whole story to recognize the full impact of the event.

Life flows in that manner, what the world sees as a small trickle will sometimes make a gushing impact. What can be overlooked by the uninformed may be one of the most monumental events to mold our lives.

Noah's best friend on the team was Antares, the quarterback. As their inaugural season progressed, they connected several times on pass plays. Noah celebrated the catches, and he felt the disappointment of the drops as well. He learned the joy and heartache of this game called football. But he kept practicing, kept going back to the huddle—whether he touched the ball or not—and one day it finally happened: Antares threw the ball thirty yards down the field. Noah trusted his practice, had learned from the drops, and caught the ball. He covered the remaining few yards of the field as quickly as his bean-pole legs could move and raced across the goal line. Touchdown! Noah and his friend Antares had teamed up to share in the celebration of giving and *receiving*.

There are similarities between the game of football and our journey in life. We have some setbacks—dropped passes along the way. But sometimes—when we least expect it, we achieve greatness—we score. Noah's first catch was a little thing, like Carver and Karen's small acts for Chucky. The touchdown was a big thing, like the Phillips' willingness to take in Chucky as if he were a birth child. Both are important. It takes the little things—five-yard outs—and the big things—touchdowns—to achieve fulfillment in the game and life. May we be willing to give and receive, the large and the small, and in the process exemplify the grace of a great *receiver* named Chucky Mullins.

Chucky with Carver, Karen, Lamar and Keshia Phillips

15: ANGER

NURSE JUDY WAS LOUD AND BOSSY. KAREN HAD NOTICED THAT ON more than one occasion she was a little rough with Chucky's motionless body. This action by Judy was not meant to be mean or intentional. She was just so busy and energetic that she failed to understand the importance of a gentle spirit. Some caregivers have the ability to enter a room like a gentle breeze, bathing their patients in the warmth of their presence. Judy barged in like a hurricane and was as comforting as a cold November rain.

Chucky began responding to Judy's entrance into his Oxford home with a masterful touch. Whenever she came into his room, he would close his eyes. Although naturally insensitive to the needs of others, Judy picked up on Chucky's signal. "He doesn't like me," she regretfully acknowledged to Karen. He communicated his displeasure without saying a harsh word.

Chucky practiced a skill that I call a "gentle-rebuke." The Bible offers a beautiful model of this principle in the gospel of Luke. Jesus is quoted there instructing his followers on how to react when they are displeased with another. He says in Luke 17:3, "So watch yourselves, if your brother sins, rebuke him, and if he repents, forgive him." Jesus offers a warning to be careful in how we respond to an offender, "So watch yourselves."

We may be angry about another's actions, but if care is not taken, we might respond in a manner similarly offensive to them. They may feel just as wronged and will become angry as well. When this happens there is little opportunity for growth or constructive correction. Before Jesus instructs his friends to rebuke, he says to be careful how they do it. In other words, he says to rebuke gently and *watch yourself.*

Chucky listened to the call of Jesus to rebuke gently. He was careful and gentle with how he corrected Judy. He let his actions—closed eyes—speak to his displeasure of Judy's behavior. It was what he didn't say that made all the difference in her life. He did not yell at her or express his frustration with *anger.* He understood the importance of stopping unpleasant behavior by the kindest way possible.

Jesus would put these principles into practice in the very next chapter of Luke's gospel. People were bringing babies to Jesus so that he could put his hands upon them and offer a blessing. The evangelist, Luke, shares that the disciples took offense at this event and rebuked those bringing the children. Jesus corrects what may have been a harsh rebuke by the disciples with a gentle rebuke of his own. He explained their misstep and instructed them on how to properly respond by telling them, "Let the children come to me, for they are the greatest in the kingdom of heaven." It seems that he did not yell and correct the disciples in a belittling manner. He corrected them gently and explained why the correction was in order.

Imagine the affirmation we would communicate to others if we applied Jesus' compassionate method of correction. Sure, our subordinates or children may be quick to stop their displeasing behavior if we yell at them. But does every incident need an aggressive response to promote a change? If the negative response continues, we will need to become more assertive through our words and actions. But can't we start with the gentlest measure of expressing our disapproval? Any good barber will tell you the most effective way to *clip the bangs* is a little at a time. You can always *take off more,* but you can't put it back once it has been cut.

When Judy started exuding a calmer spirit, Chucky started opening his eyes. Eventually their relationship became warm, and he started talking to her. Judy changed her behavior and Chucky built a more full relationship with her. The passage referenced earlier from the gospel of Luke speaks about more than healthy rebukes. Jesus' last advice was to forgive the offender when they turn from troublesome behavior. Judy had learned from Chucky's gentle rebuke and made a correction. Chucky was quick to forgive and begin a healthy relationship with another child of brokenness.

Chucky watching his Ole Miss teammates play the game

16: EXPECTATIONS

THE PASTOR READ A PASSAGE OF SCRIPTURE FROM THE OLD TESTA-
ment's Book of Exodus. The man of the cloth was a skilled orator.
He recited the sacred scripture from his King James Bible and then
retold the text, in story form, to his flock. "When the people, Israel, put their faith in God, He delivered them from slavery into the
Promised Land!"

The congregants assisted the speaker by inserting their own
comments as he spoke. With each pause for breath, he was greeted
with a response from the gathering. Some delivered a simple: *uh-
huh, yes, or speak.* Others were more assertive and wordy: "Come
on now, preacher!"

The background noise was not a distraction to the worship leader. Rather, he accepted their reaction as affirmation and encouragement for the Word being spoken to his people.

"Now listen to me, Church...some of you may feel a little like
foreigners in a weary land today. Your bondage may not be by
slave-masters from Egypt, like Israel faced. But you still feel the
heaviness of captivity in your life. Tell me, Church, are you hungry
for freedom from your own Egypt today?"

The man with the microphone stirred the congregation into a
boisterous state as they reacted to his rhetorical question. "Whoever is holding you in bondage today, whatever has you captive this
very hour, you can be set free!"

One of the matriarchs of the church cried out in her all-too-familiar shrill voice, "Yes we can, Lord!" She gave a hint of who the Deliverer was, as the minister brought the message to its climax.

"Whoever holds the whip, whatever is the slave-master in your life, there are many things that can shackle us, but there is only One who can set you free!" The pastor believed that some of his flock were victims of a broken world. But he also understood that others had created a self-inflicted subjugation. Regardless of the cause or nature of the disease, the antidote was the same.

"So come to the waters, like the people of Israel. Look to the Red Sea in front of you and gaze back over your shoulder at the attackers behind you. Believe, have faith, trust in the Lord! And He…He is the one that will part the waters and deliver you on dry land. Amen and Amen!" Exhausted, he fell back into the pulpit chair, completely spent from the miracle of grace he had encountered in speaking the holy word.

A few minutes later the pastor regained his strength and greeted the congregation as they departed the house of worship. A particularly strong woman, known as Mae Jane to her friends and Muh to her grandkids, approached him. "Mrs. Mullins, it was so good seeing you in God's house today. You are indeed a pillar upon which this church stands."

She calmly acknowledged the comment with thanksgiving and encouraged her grandson to extend his hand. "Chucky, tell Pastor how much you enjoyed his message today."

The little one had not reached double digits in age, but he had sat through more sermons than most people twice his years. As one transitioning from baby to permanent eating tools, he burst into a toothless smile and proclaimed, "I enjoyed it, Pastor!"

The family always gathered for Sunday lunch at Muh's house after worship. On this particular day, she felt a growling in her soul to digest the day's sermon, along with the noonday meal. "Y'all heard Pastor speak about the Israelites crossing the Red Sea, didn't you?"

They answered with all the respect their grandmother had earned and demanded, "Yes, Ma'am!"

Having gained their attention, she continued, "Just a few days after walking across the Red Sea they were grumbling to Moses and the Lord. God had given them food and water in the desert so they could survive. But the people complained saying the food was too bland and the water was too scarce. Why do you think they complained?" Like any good teacher she peppered her lesson with questions, not just answers, so that she and her students could arrive at the answer together.

"They were spoiled," one said.

"They didn't appreciate what they had," another offered.

Their matriarch celebrated their answers and moved them to the deeper truth. "The Lord provided several miracles to get them out of bondage in Egypt. Maybe they took His grace for granted and thought that once He delivered them, it would be smooth sailing?" She offered the central point as a suggestion rather than a dominant proclamation. Allowing the children to use their own minds for reflection and not simply mimic her beliefs. Then she told the children, "They had seen God work miracles for their *survival*, and they wanted the same miracles for their *comfort*. I think they started grumbling because they had raised their *expectations* too high."

Muh had the floor in this follow-up sermon. The kitchen table was her pulpit. The background noise was no longer a house of worshipers but the clink of silverware. She was not a preacher, but the message was just as powerful as that of her pastor. "The Lord doesn't owe you anything, and the world sho' ain't gonna give you nothing. Life is not always fair."

She paused to pass the collard greens, symbolizing her desire to nurture the body and soul of her loved ones. "The Good Book says that the Lord allows it to rain a little on the good and the bad folk.

No matter who you are, it ain't always gonna be easy. We all have deserts to walk through, but when we walk with the Lord, it's easier than if we walked alone." She ended her homily by summarizing a Christian poem titled, *Footprints in the Sand*. "He takes every step with us in the desert, even when we feel like we are alone. If you ever look back and there ain't but one set of tracks, don't think He has left you—that's when He's carrying you. I hope you never forget that, my precious babies."

It is now the fall of 1990, and Chucky is sitting alone with his thoughts. These days he has ample time to reminisce about happier times. Later in the afternoon, Chucky will conduct one of the countless interviews that he has given since his injury. But for now his thoughts are reflecting upon his childhood and the tutelage of his grandmother.

When the sports columnist arrived he was eager to understand how Chucky responded to adversity with such a positive attitude. Chucky offered him a glimpse into his past saying, "I have been through hardships before; I understand life is not easy."

The journalist was inspired by Chucky's mindset but wondered if the competitor ever had downtimes. "Sure, I've cried a lot of times," Chucky said, his baritone voice uttering each word in harmony. "But I never felt sorry for myself. And I don't want anyone to feel sorry for me."

The interviewer saw in this young man an honesty and wisdom beyond his years. But of course, anyone who knew Chucky's teacher from long ago would not have been surprised by his responses. Mrs. Mary Jane Mullins poured the water of life into Chucky and an *expectation* to persevere through whatever dry land he traversed.

In his paralysis, Chucky could no longer walk on this earth or through the sands of his own desert. But he kept moving–pressing forward toward the Promised Land. There was only one set of tracks now as Chucky journeyed, and he never forgot Who was carrying him.

17: FAITH

IN JANUARY 1983, CHUCKY MULLINS WAS THIRTEEN YEARS OLD. HE
and his sixteen-year old brother, Horace, were being raised in a
single parent home by their mother, Linda. Sadly, pneumonia in-
fected Linda's lungs and left her critically ill.

Chucky and Horace had different fathers and neither had been
active in their son's lives. Karen Phillips was a distant relative of
Horace's and Carver had coached him in recreational basketball.
The Phillips knew that the Mullins boys were alone at home while
their mother was slowly smothering to death in the hospital. Carver and Karen stopped by the family apartment and checked on the
boys a couple of times. Linda Mullins drew her last weak breath
on January 26, 1983. Her mother, Mary Jane Mullins, had been
the rock of the family before dying a few years prior to Linda. The
passing of these two women left the boys with no immediate family
to give them a home.

Horace and Chucky were placed in foster care and did not adjust well. Their new caregiver was not a sports fan and discouraged
the boys' participation in athletics. After a few weeks under the care
appointed by the state, the Mullins boys were ready for a change.
Chucky Mullins had felt the temporary care and compassion offered by Carver and Karen Phillips. Now he was hopeful that they
would take up the job in a full-time capacity.

The Phillips were eating dinner one evening when the rectangle-shaped kitchen phone sounded its bell-toned alarm. The vibration on the wood paneling wall foreshadowed how their world was about to be shaken to the core. "Hey, this is Chucky."

Carver answered with his natural warm and charismatic reply, "Hey, buddy, how you doin', man?"

Chucky did not mince his words and got right to the point. "Not too good. We don't really like it here."

Carver pulled the green cord as far as he could away from the background noise of the dinner table as the conversation grew serious. "What's wrong, man?"

"They put us with Ms. Dale. She's a good lady, but she don't want us to play sports."

Horace was the superior athlete of the Mullins kids, but Carver saw in Chucky a passion for athletics that few possessed. "Aw, Chucky, I hate to hear that." He understood that Chucky saw football as the one thing that would help him escape to a better life.

"Can we come stay with y'all?"

There was little else said, and the conversation ended as abruptly as it had started. At the age of 13, Chucky had no skill or inclination for small talk. He had gotten down to the business of his life, and there was nothing more to say. As soon as Carver returned the phone to its rotary base, he shared the conversation with Karen. The parents, with a combined age of less than fifty years, were now faced with a life-altering decision.

Twenty years prior, Karen Phillips went through a traumatic family transition of her own and empathized with the boys' pain. Karen was just two when her family was broken apart by divorce. Karen and her three-year-old sister, Linda, remained in the custody of their father Bobby.

Raising two young girls as a single parent was a daunting task. The dad soon found himself ill-equipped to meet all of the girls' needs. His parents, Otha and Nannie Graham, came to the rescue, offering unlimited assistance and stability. Eventually, the family realized that the healthiest option would be for the two young girls to move into the home of their paternal grandparents.

The matriarch of the family was a lovable soul who nurtured the girls with a mother's heart. She was a devoted Christian who gave Karen the seeds of the faith to carry her throughout her life. "Karen, what do you think about that scripture that says, *If you have faith as small as a mustard seed, you can move a mountain?*"

"I think it tells us that we need a lot of faith," Karen responded.

Nannie Graham encouraged Karen's response and added to it, "Amen! It also says that *nothing is impossible with faith.* I am glad that it says if you have just a *little* faith, small as a mustard seed. That's not a very big seed, child."

She ended with a treasure that Karen has never forgotten. "Sometimes it's hard to have *big* faith. In times like that, I like to remember: *It's not how big your FAITH is, but how big is the GOD that you have faith in.*"

Now Karen was calling on the wisdom of her grandmother to provide insight regarding Chucky and Horace. In addition to the Mullins kids, she and Carver had their own young babies to consider. Three-year-old Lamar and two-year-old Keshia would surely have to sacrifice if the number of children in the household doubled overnight [Carver also has a daughter named Christy that did not live in his home; she was nine years old at the time].

It was not lost upon Karen that her children were the exact age as she and her sister were when the makeup of their family changed—two and three years old. Karen knew that her upbringing had not held to a traditional family structure, but it had been good. Nannie Graham had embraced her with love, overcoming any wants she might have known.

As Karen considered her own kids, she could not stop thinking about the two boys who needed a home. She was grateful that her grandparents took her in at a fragile age and felt a conviction to share what she had been given. She felt sure that her grandmother had planted enough love in her heart for four children and not just two. Carver and Karen had agreed to "sleep on it" overnight. But the truth is, Karen's heart had already made the decision before her head hit the pillow that night. The boys were getting a new home.

Karen looks back now with amusement at the tough times. "People thought we were crazy taking in those teenage boys when we had two babies of our own."

They were given some governmental assistance for the financial load. Each child received a check in the amount of $120 per month for personal needs. In addition, the Phillips received $60 per month to assist with the added cost that the Mullins boys placed upon their household. Karen remembers with a laugh, "Sixty dollars doesn't go very far with growing boys. They could eat up sixty dollars a week in groceries."

The Phillips were aware that some foster parents utilized a portion of the children's money to assist with the larger family cost. Karen and Carver never considered that plan and explained their formula in simple terms, "We told the boys to keep their money to spend as they saw fit. We bought all the food, paid all the bills, and placed no financial burden upon Horace or Chucky."

In 1993, The Phillips household expanded again when they were asked to take care of a two-month-old baby named Ramono Craig. Ramono never left the home and embraced the Phillips as his family with the same enthusiasm as Chucky. Although Ramono never knew Chucky personally, he wore Chucky's football numbers 2 and 38. Ramono understood, like his brother Chucky before him, that being part of the Phillips family was not limited to birth children.

Karen never regretted the decision to make the little boys in need a part of their family. Although the money supplied by the government was never enough, they had an additional source of strength rooted in the words of Nannie Graham, "If you have *faith* as small as a mustard seed, you can move mountains."

Nannie Graham planted seeds of *faith* in Karen Phillips. As Karen nurtured her extended family, some of these seeds of faith fell into Chucky's path as well. It was this *faith* that matured in the fertile soil of Chucky Mullins and continues to produce fruit to this day.

The Karen and Carver Phillips family in 2014, pictured from the left: Karen and Carver, Kylie and Christy, Lamar and Cahlese, Keshia and P. J. with Kalesha and Antoyia, Ramono and Raylon, Aleshia with Chucky's picture inside the Manning Center at Ole Miss.

18: WORK

CARVER AND KAREN PHILLIPS ENSURED THAT CHUCKY AND HIS brother Horace would have a loving home after their mother's death. In addition to the Phillips, there were other gracious souls in the Russellville community who nurtured Chucky's life.

With the move into the Phillips' household, Chucky was able to resume his love of playing football. One of his coaches during those Pee-Wee football years was Tommy James. Coach James would drive Chucky to and from practice anytime he needed a ride. He also provided Chucky with an additional male role model that had been lacking in his early years.

Chucky's main mode of transportation, like many young people in the early eighties, was a bicycle. During this same era, it was customary for gasoline to be sold at garages known as *filling stations*. Unlike today's gas stations, these businesses pumped the gas *for you* and supplied full service auto care.

Donny Seale was the owner and operator of a local filling station, and Chucky was a frequent patron. The Mullins kid was familiar to Mr. Seale because he was a classmate of his daughter, Deedra. Although it wasn't a car, Donny worked on Chucky's bike countless times to keep him peddling and smiling all over town. Donny Seale never accepted payment for his services because contributing to Chucky's journey through Russellville and beyond was payment enough.

Mr. David Sibley was a local businessman who allowed a young

Chucky to *work* at his establishment to earn a little extra spending money. On one occasion, Chucky's boss asked him to clean the bathroom at one of his convenience stores. The manager of the store got busy, forgetting about Chucky and the assigned task. More than an hour passed when the boss walked into the restroom for his personal needs.

Upon entering the restroom, he was startled to see Chucky standing on a step ladder. He was cleaning the light fixture attached to the ceiling. His employer and advocate asked, "What are you doing?"

Chucky replied, "I already done the commode, sink, and floor. I was just trying to get these bugs out of the light fixture."

Nobody told him to quit so he just kept working. This event was a precursor to how Chucky would respond to every task he took on in life. When he began a project, he would go until he couldn't go any more or until someone stopped him. It was this commitment of hard *work* that was foundational to his motto: *Never Quit.*

Periodically, I attend a prayer retreat center near Brooksville, Mississippi, called The Dwelling Place. On one occasion, the founder, Clare Van Lent, told me how they often receive timely gifts when needs are the greatest. This deep woman of faith attributed the results to devout prayer and trusting in God.

I asked in a respectful tone, "Is that all you do? Pray?"

She responded quickly, "No! I ask everyone that I know to partner with us, I write for grants, we host fund raising events, and we work tirelessly."

She finally took a breath and paused for effect before saying, "We pray like everything depends on God; we *work* like everything depends on us."

The balance of faith and *work* applied to Chucky as well. I mentioned in the prior chapter how he began his pursuit for success by trusting in God with faith. He continued by putting his faith in action with hard *work*. Seeds of faith had been planted into his life by others. But, like any good gardener, Chucky understood that he had to also *work* the ground to promote growth.

The Pee Wee football coach, Tommy James, always made an effort to get Chucky on the team that he coached. It wasn't because Chucky was the best player in the league, at times he wasn't even the most talented athlete on his own team. But Coach James saw a quality in Chucky that was unsurpassed by any young person he had met.

Coach James explained it this way, "There were more talented players in our league, but nobody *wanted it* more than Chucky. He used every ounce of ability there was inside of that small body. I think he had visions of improving his life through football—that's why he wanted it." Many people share Chucky's *desire* for a better life; what set him apart was his willingness to *work* for it with equal enthusiasm.

In later years, his *work* ethic never changed throughout his days as a high school and college football player. One of his teammates on the Russellville High School football team was named Wade Sumerel. He witnessed Chucky's *work* effort in high school and is still inspired by it today. Wade remembers, "He is the only guy that I ever played with who liked to practice as much as playing in the games."

Don Cox was the head coach for Chucky's high school team. He shared how Chucky exerted himself on the field, "He would hit other players so hard in practice that we had to tell him to dial it back a notch. He was full speed all the time, he didn't know half speed. You weren't gonna out-*work* him, but he made it fun out there too."

Years before Chucky's efforts on the high school football field, his *work* ethic was on display as he cleaned the restroom. Chucky could have stopped after bringing a sparkle to the toilet and sink that day. He didn't know for sure what to do next so he just kept working. He went on to clean the floor and then the ceiling as well. His climb up the ladder in the restroom was symbolic of how his commitment to *work* helped him rise above challenges.

Chucky's attitude was this, *when the chips are down and times are tough let's just WORK as hard as we can and see what happens.* I don't think Chucky was so naïve as to believe *work* offered a fail-proof formula. However, he understood that he could not accomplish any endeavor if he didn't at least *work* at it.

The good people of Russellville, Alabama, were the first to witness Chucky Mullins' strong *work* ethic, which inspired them to also *work* on his behalf. Coach Don Cox describes the relationship this way, "He was special to us here in Russellville long before he went to Ole Miss. He always cared about other people, I'm sure that is one of the reasons we cared so much for him."

19: CHOICES

"CHUCKY, YOU KNOW BY THE TIME WE GET TO THE SKATING RINK all the fine girls gon' be talking to somebody already?" Horace directed this rhetorical comment in Chucky's direction. Though technically a question, Horace presented it more like an accusation, an opening statement in which Chucky had to prove himself innocent, or at least argue his way out.

"Yeah, man, I wish we could be there when it starts," Chucky said with only a minor touch of heartache, unaware where his brother planned to take this conversation.

Horace pressed on, "Well, we could be there at the start if we didn't have to go to church first every dad-gum Wednesday night." He was careful to make the enemy in this battle the Wednesday night church event itself and not the leaders of the Phillip's household. Aware of Chucky's loyalty to Carver and Karen, he excluded them from his assault until the very end. Without giving Chucky time to fully recover from these verbal jabs, Horace went for the knock-out: "Let's just tell 'em we're not going." There! He said it, limited his words, did not address the authorities by name, got to the point...*let's don't go!*

Chucky instinctively reacted, "Man, Carver and Karen ain't gonna let us skip church." The difference was in the wording. Horace called it an innocent *not going*. Chucky said what it was to him—*skipping*.

The big brother asserted his authority, "Just let me do the talking, I think I can get 'em. They don't own us anyway. We just staying here." Chucky was out of the words or energy to respond. Now he was just listening to his brother lead them down a path that would forever change their lives.

Certain events occur in all of our lives to inspire the belief that a given outcome was our destiny. To be sure, life is indeed influenced by circumstances and events that we do not control. But the ultimate result of our individual existence on earth is significantly impacted by the *choices* we make as well. Surely our reactions to those events that are beyond our power to control are deeply foundational to the direction of life's road. In other words, the *choices* we make matter as much or more than the circumstances that choose us.

So the *choice* was made on a fateful Wednesday, and the consequences were quick to follow. Carver and Karen busied themselves with their routine preparation as their departure time was nearing. The boys, however, remained motionless, acting as though they had already had the conversation, and it was a unanimous decision by all voting members that they would not attend church that evening.

Karen finally broke the silence, "Y'all ready to go?" Her introduction was just as effective as Horace's spoken hours earlier to Chucky, similarly short but full of assumption and finality. She did not have to state where they were going for that had been determined several years ago.

Carver and Karen meant it when they joined their lives *with* God in holy matrimony. They believed that the essential ingredient for a successful relationship was to include the Creator in the recipe. They were not about to try and nourish the souls of their extended family of four kids without His help now.

"We ain't goin'." Horace made an effort to express this statement in a manner that would limit the offense as much as possible. It wasn't just him. Chucky and he were together in this decision.

Giving him a chance to backup or withdraw his motion, Karen firmly asked, "What was that, Horace?"

He knew quickly that it was not going well so he softened his comments a bit, "We going skating this week." He limited it to a one-week offense. It wasn't so much a rejection of where they weren't going: *church*. It was a commitment to where they were going: *skating*.

But Karen did not interpret it as a subtle statement and did not waiver in her commitment even when caught off-guard. "That's not an option. Everybody who stays in this house goes to church when they're supposed to."

Chucky was looking down, trying to remove himself from this confrontation in any way that he could. But there was no escape plan written on the top of his sneakers. A shot had been fired, sides had been chosen, and he had to make a stand with one or the other.

Carver tried to defuse the escalating tension, saying "Man, y'all know we go to church as a family. We always let y'all go skating after church."

Karen joined Carver's extension of the olive branch as she softened her voice and offered reassurance. "Guys, we want y'all here, but if you're gonna stay, you gotta live by the same rules we all do." She masterfully expressed her affection for the boys, while making it clear that affection does not preclude the need for discipline in a family.

The Phillips believed that real love is always equipped with the hard stuff as well. Sometimes the most loving thing a parent can say to a kid is "*no*." They held firm that a family, or any institution, would crumble without rules, discipline, and consequences.

When we live out our love in this manner it is sometimes called "tough love." Some interpret that to mean that those in authority make it "tough" on the recipient of our love when we lace it with structure and rules. But those with nurturing hearts, like Karen and Carver, find it equally tough to administer this kind of necessary love. It is much easier to always say yes—be the good guys—and strive for unrelenting friendship with those entrusted to our care. But that was not real love in the mind of these young parents of faith.

"Come on, bro, we gotta go!" Horace took command with these words. He agreed with Karen's statement that family sticks together. But in his mind, he was only part of a family of two.

So Horace and Chucky packed up the items they needed for the journey in a matching set of paper sacks from the local Piggly Wiggly grocery store. The *choice* that would forever change their lives had been made. Once they walked out the door, things would never be the same.

20: ALONE

CHUCKY CROSSED OVER THE THRESHOLD OF THE PHILLIPS' HOME BE-cause this is what kinfolk do. Family has a natural inclination to stick together when other relationships fall apart. No special words have to be spoken. Instead, there is comfort in knowing that we are in it together—we're not *alone*.

As they walked farther away from the Phillips' home, Horace used fewer words to complement their journey. Chucky sensed the plan's failure almost immediately. There was no clear path of where they were going beyond the skating rink. Neither had Chucky received a game plan for where they would be staying. Had Chucky been a music fan of the legendary country singer Merle Haggard, the following words would have rang prophetically in his ears: *I can make it for a day or two without you...but what am I gonna do for the rest of my life?*

Many of us have chosen similar paths for certain journeys in life. We have a deep hunger to run toward something new, or away from something old. But beyond our appetite for change we fail to consider the cost of the journey. In the days ahead, Chucky's internal itch, *suspecting* that this was a bad choice, would grow into an absolute outbreak of *knowing* it was a poor decision. He soon wished he had not left home and brought this added grief upon himself.

Carver was employed at a local factory and often worked the evening shift. On many occasions, he would catch a glimpse of

Chucky hanging around outside on the street as he left the neighborhood. "He would be out there on the street corner talking to his friends every time that I passed," Carver recalled. It wasn't clear if Chucky's primary motivation was to be with his friends or to be seen by Carver. It's doubtful that Chucky was familiar with the writings of 15th century author Thomas à Kempis, who is credited by some for originating the statement, "Out of sight, out of mind." But it appears that Chucky had considered this option and was not taking any chances.

When the "be seen" strategy failed to inspire the desired result, Chucky took to the influence of a modern-day creator of food and phrases, Emeril Lagasse, and "kicked it up a notch." This more aggressive tactic would entail the assistance of a third-party collaborator. He approached a young girl at school who lived next door to Carver and Karen and asked her, "Hey, will you ask them if I can come home?"

Horace had made it clear to Chucky and the Phillips that he was a man now at the ripe old age of 16 and would not be returning. Chucky felt the same passion as Horace, but his was turned in the opposite direction. As a young teenager, Chucky knew where home was, and it was the Phillips' house.

Time is a funny thing. While participating in a dreaded activity, the seconds seem to creep by. However, when we are happy, time is ignored and passes by unaccounted. The twenty-four hours from Chucky's request to the response was one of those slow times.

After an evening of restless sleep, his judgment time mercifully came the next morning at school. Chucky saw his messenger and made a bee-line in her direction. If he was a bee then she carried herself like the queen of these flying insects. He wasn't sure if she would bring honey or a sting, but he had to know.

Upon his arrival at her side it was instantly evident who would be in charge of these proceedings. He didn't even extend his request before she offered her wordless response. All his anticipation hedged on the movement of the child's head. With two swift jerks of her noggin— one to the left, the other to the right—his hopes were dashed.

This became an everyday routine for Chucky and the Queen Bee. She would deliver the sting that must have felt like a shot to his heart with each injection. But Chucky insisted on taking this daily dose of medicine every morning at school.

"He sho' is pitiful, Ms. Karen. He keeps asking every day. I told him he was making my stomach hurt askin' so much. I said, won't you just let me tell you if she changes her mind? He said he would try, but sure enough first time he sees me he asks again."

It certainly would have been simpler, and perhaps less painful, if Chucky had taken the advice of his young courier. But he maintained his daily routine of consistent interrogation. He felt compelled to face the music that his choice had orchestrated. So he kept asking and she kept answering.

Chucky had experienced more intense emotional pain from the loss of his mother and grandmother. But his present predicament was different because he had made the choice that brought about his current hardship. In other words, most of the peril he faced early in life was uninvited and cast upon his innocent shoulders. But this feeling of emptiness sprang from a burden that he brought upon himself.

There seems to be extra pain when we create our own harsh circumstances. So Chucky took ownership of his plight and worked hard to overcome it.

Karen was unusually quiet one evening as Carver was preparing to leave for work. He asked if something was wrong. "You know what's wrong," she answered.

"Yeah, I know. You think it's time?" He was careful to ask and not suggest.

"I miss him terribly, Carver. You think he has learned his lesson?" They were both asking questions and searching for the right answer.

So, after weeks of the same response, the carrier offered a twist in her delivery. As Chucky approached, her days of using sign language were over. She could not hold back her enthusiasm, yelling, "She said yes!"

Don't we all know his response? Could he have expressed his reaction in any other way? You guessed it....he smiled.

The dedicated young messenger would later tell Karen, "I know he smiles a lot, but he was grinning from ear to ear every time I saw him for the whole rest of the day."

Karen may have relented to assist the girl as well as Chucky. The young lady had become quite an effective promoter of the underdog's cause. Chucky had that effect upon others throughout his life. People unwittingly found themselves rooting for this guy. It was hard not to be on his side and even harder not to like him. Chucky was a winner, and doesn't everyone like to be on the side of a winner?

Two weeks had lapsed since Chucky deserted the Phillips' home. It could have been much shorter, or a little longer, but for Chucky it was an eternal lesson, one that he would not forget for the rest of his life.

Karen and Carver recalled they never had a bit of trouble after that "vacation" from home. "Well, there was that one thing," they say now with laughter. "He and one of his little friends took a city truck for a joy ride." Carver explained the consequences of that event in detail, "One of my friends worked in the district attorney's office, and he put the fear in Chucky. He took him for a ride to the juvenile center and asked, 'Do you want to be here in 'Juvie' or in the good home Carver and Karen gave you?'"

It's clear that Chucky did not always make the right choices. He was a typical young person and made bad decisions, mistakes we all commit. The extraordinary thing about Chucky was that he was a superior student in the classroom of life. He learned from his mistakes and the bad choices that were the cause.

So Carver and Karen welcomed Chucky back into the Phillips' household. The first evening home, little was said but much was communicated. Chucky's favorite dish—rice—was served in abundance, complemented by a side of smiles offered by all. Their reason for taking Chucky back can be explained with the same words that began this chapter: *Chucky crossed over the threshold of the Phillips' home because this is what kinfolk do. Family has a natural inclination to stick together when other relationships fall apart. No special words have to be spoken. Instead, there is comfort in knowing that we are in it together—we're not ALONE.*

21: HERO

THE FINAL SCORE ON THE BOARD READ HOME 20, VISITORS 21. IT was a devastating loss for the guys in black and gold.

The home team had set a school record of 14 wins during the season, but this one loss was for all the marbles—the state championship.

Now it was ALL over. Their brilliant season—finished. The hope of providing their hometown with a championship—vanished. The seniors' joy in wearing a high school football uniform—gone.

While exiting the stadium, a fifth grader named Matt walked by the locker room with his dad and gazed inside. He gawked like a rubbernecker who sees an ambulance at the scene of an automobile crash. Matt suspected that the inner sanctum of the dressing room would not be a pleasant image, but he couldn't help but look.

Most of the Golden Tigers football team was kneeling with tears in their eyes. It seemed that they were all filled with emotions except for *one*, and he was wearing number *two* on his chest.

Whether it had been choreographed or was a natural response, the wounded warriors of the gridiron had assembled around their leader. He was standing while his teammates were kneeling. He offered no tears or raw emotions as he shouldered the loss.

Matt and his father made the cold walk to the parking lot in record time. As they entered the quiet of the pickup truck, number two was still on the mind of the eleven year old. "Why was Chucky not crying, Dad?"

The kid with *Mullins* written on the back of his jersey had inspired fans of Russellville High throughout his career. So the father answered his son's question without a second thought. "Chucky has nothing to cry about because he left it all on the field."

Chucky was a leader in the dad's eyes, but to young Matt he had become something more. He was Matt's *hero*. Before the vehicle's interior had warmed up, Matt made a vow to himself. *He would never give himself a reason to cry after a game.*

No one attains hero status by solely accomplishing greatness on the field of play. To be enthroned with that honor you have to be liked by the commoners. It was when Matt received the royal treatment several weeks prior that Chucky was crowned his *hero*.

The setting for the coronation was fifth grade PE class. It began as a typical day, with much chatter among the pupils. The coach got everyone's attention with one blow of the whistle. "Boys, we have a special guest coach today."

Chucky Mullins walked into the gathering of the future Golden Tigers. Matt had his tube socks stretched securely in place, all the way to the top of his knees. He was ready to do battle on the kickball field and his competitive instincts kicked in gear, "I've got Chucky on my team!"

Matt knew all about Chucky's accomplishments as a star athlete. He attended every Russellville football game with his dad, even when they were away games. Matt understood that he was in the presence of greatness.

The coach introduced his former student for those who were not as familiar with his talents. "Chucky wants to be a coach one day, but I am not sure he would be very good at it," the coach joked at Chucky's expense. "Chucky won't ever be able to correct his players when they mess up because he's always smiling." The coach made it clear that he was kidding and displayed his affection for this special young man. "Nope, he won't be a *good* coach; he will be a *great* coach! I am proud that I had the opportunity to teach him, and I hope he can one day coach some of you."

Chucky didn't do much coaching with Matt and his friends that day. Instead, he laced up his shoes tight and played with the youngsters. At break time he laughed with the goofy pre-teens as if all their silly attempts at humor were funny.

Chucky was the biggest man on campus at the high school. But here he was lowering himself to the level of the little guys in fifth grade. He didn't take himself too seriously or his new friends too lightly. This is where the transformation from great player to *hero* occurred for Chucky. Not on the football field but on the kickball field.

Some players influence the game with a winning effort. H*eroes* are committed to making those around them winners, too. Others go so far as to achieve greatness on the field, while *heroes* inspire greatness in others. Some players are leaders whom others like and want to follow. A *hero* is one whom others love and want to emulate. Great coaches encourage discipline in their players, while *heroes* inspire devotion from their teammates and fans.

Chucky's career did not end on that cold evening when his team lost their last high school football game. He would go on to attain the victory of playing football in the SEC. The *hero* went off to college, and Matt would move to another town a few years later, but he never forgot the impact of Chucky Mullins. Chucky had sparked a desire for greatness in Matt. He kept working even when times were hard because he wanted to grow up and play SEC football like Chucky.

In 1995, Matt Wyatt's dream became a reality when he was awarded a scholarship to play football for the Mississippi State University Bulldogs. He would go on to become a starting quarterback in the greatest football conference in the land: the SEC. I suspect he became a *hero* himself to some fifth-graders along the way.

I once had lunch at a diner where the servers wore buttons that read I'm number 2.

Curiosity got the best of me, and I inquired about it.

My waitress answered with excitement that conveyed, I thought you would never ask, "I'm number 2 because you're number 1!"

I'm sure Chucky never ate at that restaurant. Yet he embodied their commitment to wear number two. But he also lived the number, and in the process became a *hero* in the eyes of those he made number one. I am grateful that Matt Wyatt replicated Chucky's winning attitude and continued Russellville, Alabama's heroic contribution in the state of Mississippi.

22: GOOD

THE MOST ANXIOUS DAY OF THE LITTLE LEAGUE BASEBALL SEASON had arrived. Although the first game was still weeks away, the head coach was already feeling the pressure of being the skipper. It was time to select the numbers that would adorn the uniforms of his eleven-year-old players.

The coach had instituted a fair process for the number-picking extravaganza. He would send out a mass text message to each parent on the team. The instructions were simple and diplomatic, "Send me a text with your son's number request. If it is the first request that I receive for that specific number, then it is his."

It was a mad scramble to see who could text the fastest. The process was intensified by the creativity of several players. A social-clique named "the four horsemen" had chosen a sequence of numbers to represent their team-within-the-team. One meddlesome kid or a spiteful parent could mess up their master plan of securing numbers 9, 10, 11, and 12.

The coach's phone had been blowing up during the hour of negotiations, but the roster was finally complete. He took a deep breath and relaxed from the exhaustion of the event. He recollected that, all things considered, it went pretty well. No one had gotten so frustrated with the number grab that he had left the team.

Later in the evening he would receive a call from a parent he had overlooked. *Oh no!* His emotions went into a reflexive overload. Had he forgotten to include the family in the mass text? How would he explain that all of the *good* numbers had already been chosen? No single digits left. Now the number saga would continue. He could not run forever, not answering the phone, so he decided to take it like a man.

Moments after his *hello*, the coach's fear was confirmed. He had one more number to assign. "Hi, Coach, this is Trea calling to give you Alden's number."

The coach was taken aback a bit at how the conversation had begun. This poor fellow didn't realize a parent doesn't just call up and automatically receive a sought-after number. "I'm sorry, Trea, but everyone else has already selected a number. I hope we can find a number that Alden will be happy with."

The dad did not respond in the manner that the coach was hoping for. "Well, Alden will only be happy with one number."

The coach thought to himself, *Can you believe the nerve of this guy? He waits until the battle for the numbers is over to make the call. Then he has the gumption to say, "He will only be happy with one number."*

But the coach restrained himself and did not show his annoyance, which was a good thing because the dad explained his position clearly in the next statement.

"I don't think it will be a problem securing my son's number. It's not really a baseball number. But Alden and his eight-year-old little brother, Weston, both choose the same number every year. Do you have number 38 available?"

In the fall of 1992, Trea Southerland became the third person to wear Number 38 as an Ole Miss Rebel in honor of Chucky Mullins. Now his two sons select the same number for each sport in which they compete. It is their way of saying that they are proud of their dad. It's also a celebration of the spirit of the original Number 38.

Trea Southerland only wore Chucky's number for one season, but he has been impacted by their friendship for a lifetime. He said, "My life would be much different today without Chucky. At the depths of life's challenges when things are really bad, I think of him and realize that it could be worse. He knew so many hardships in life. But he remained joyful and always found the silver lining to tap into."

Chucky inspired Trea to see that even the darkest clouds have a silver lining. This is a reminder that there is some light, if we look for it, in the bleakest of circumstances. The better I understand Chucky's legacy, the more I believe that this was not an accident.

Some of us have the capacity to *believe* that God works for *good* in everything. But more than *believing,* Chucky Mullins *looked* for the *good* in everything.

In 1988, Tom Luke completed a stellar career as a high school quarterback in Gulfport, Mississippi. He was chosen to represent his home state in the inaugural Alabama – Mississippi All-Star Football Game.

Late in the contest, the Mississippi squad was trailing 7-0 with 4:26 left to play. It was then that Luke completed a 57-yard touchdown pass to tie the score.

The game went into overtime and emotions became intense. As victory hung in the balance, each competitor felt the pressure and pride of representing his home state. Luke's heroics were displayed again in the second overtime of the historic game. The quarterback scrambled for 19 yards on a dazzling run, deep into the Alabama territory. He was eventually tackled on a hard hit at the 6-yard line by a defensive back from Alabama.

As Luke rose from the ground, the tackler slapped him on the backside and yelled at him. Luke instinctively turned around to face the defender in retaliation for the disrespect.

The Alabama defender raised his fist first and Luke prepared to exchange blows. But the hand opened wide in a gesture to offer Luke a high-five. A big smile was seen on the other side of the face-mask as the defender said, "*Good* run, Ole Miss!" This was Tom Luke's first meeting with Chucky Mullins. Luke thought in that brief moment, *this must be a GOOD guy.*

Years later, Luke recalled that first meeting with his future Ole Miss teammate with clarity. But more impactful than the initial hit was the lasting impression that Chucky made upon Luke. It was the manner in which Chucky responded to his paralysis that Luke still feels today. "I remember visiting him after he got hurt, and if you didn't see the wheelchair, you would never have known anything was wrong. He really was a *good* person."

No one would say that Chucky's injury was a *good* thing. But he worked through this bad event to make *good* come from it. He became a model for teammates like Tom Luke and Trea Southerland, demonstrating how to respond to the harshest adversities with class and courage.

When we reconsider the baseball number grab that this chapter began with, it seems that the little league coach was right. All of the *good* numbers, in the eyes of most, had been taken. But the Southerland boys had the imagination to transform number 38 into a *good* number. Somehow they drew strength from the original 38, just like their dad. I guess you could say, the apple truly does not fall very far from the tree. I, too, have tasted the fruit of Chucky Mullins' inspiration, and in the words of my teammate, Tom Luke, I found it to be *good.*

23: STRENGTH

THE FOOTBALL CLEATS ARE LACED AS TIGHT AS THEY CAN BE TIED. Wrist-bands are in place with the cool logo turned in the proper direction for all to see. There is just one final addition to the uniform for this rookie football player. He gazes into a mirror and places the tape called "eye-black" on the upper cheeks of his face. The disposable tattoo on the right cheek appears to have a person's name written upon it, while on the left side there is a strange arrangement of three numbers. When it's read together the following message is communicated: "Phil 4:13."

The player preparing to do battle on this day is my ten-year-old son, Luke. This will be his first official game of little league football. He selected the eye-black because that is what the *"big boys"* do. It has become fashionable to promote this combination of name and numbers, in some manner, upon one's uniform. It can be seen in professional, college, high school and, yes, city-park leagues around the nation. Little do I know that in less than an hour my heart will break as his football career comes to an apparent end.

To the casual observer, the following questions may arise: who is Phil, what happens at 4:13, and is it a.m. or p.m.? But we live in the age of Google and smart-phones. Thus, puzzling questions do not go unanswered for very long. A quick entry into any Internet search engine will reveal the answer to this riddle in short order. Philippians 4:13 is a verse found in the New Testament portion of the Bible, which reads, "I can do all things through Christ who strengthens me."

This quote is from a letter written by a man named Paul to the Christian church in the city of Philippi. Many current-era athletes have grasped hold of these words as a call to victory: *I can win the championship; I can be all-league; I can make the team, when I rely on the strength of Christ.*

There is certainly truth in this logic for those who are followers of Jesus. But when read in the context of Paul's life in the first century, we find something more. It is not so much about achieving victory on the playing field as it is surviving defeat in life. Paul's faith inspired in him a refusal to be conquered by whatever forces he faced.

Let's forget for a moment that he was the most influential missionary to the fledgling Christian church. Yes, he would write the majority of the New Testament, but he was also in a battle for his very existence.

At the height of his occupational success, Paul went through a career change and transformation in his faith. He was a Pharisee who left his role as a prominent voice for the Jewish faith to become a promoter of the *way of Jesus.*

But this was not just a simple conversion to a new religion. Earlier in his letter to the Philippians, Paul speaks of his rich lineage in the Jewish faith. Not only had he possessed a passion for his religion, but he expressed his disdain for the emerging Christian faith by persecuting the early church (Phil 3:3). At the time of his epiphany, Paul was seen as a traitor to the Jews and as the enemy to the Christians. Thus, he was trusted by neither.

The isolation that Paul experienced must have been felt close to home as well. Surely his respect and status within his local hometown of Tarsus was ruined. I can only imagine the social stigma and embarrassment his family felt, and the pressure they must have placed upon him to relent from his "crazy" talk of a new religion.

In addition to this certain emotional and social upheaval, Paul's body was also plagued with physical unrest. He described this health challenge as a "thorn in his flesh." The Bible is not exactly clear about the details of Paul's illness, but it was clearly an unpleasant and troubling trial for Paul. It's possible he was born with some type of handicap or deformity. It is believed by some that this external hurdle presented Paul with an unusual or unattractive physical appearance.

Paul was arrested on more than one occasion for his beliefs and the practice of his ministry. During his incarceration he suffered physical abuse on multiple occasions. Few would relish interrogation or detainment by a legal authority even in today's world. But to experience such a sentence under first-century Roman rule would have been exceptionally difficult. Today, we would describe these beatings at the hands of his captors as torture.

Paul was in prison at the writing of this letter, and he referenced being in chains twice within a few short sentences. He was unjustly punished in a manner that far surpassed his supposed misdeeds. Paul would eventually be killed in a horrific manner for his missionary zeal.

Paul certainly did not enjoy the extravagant lifestyle experienced by some of today's famous athletes who promote his call to faith. He was a man plagued with challenges, rejection, pain, embarrassment, abuse, and isolation. Imagine being shackled in a dungeon, unable to grasp even a small writing instrument. Yet this was the setting in which he found himself at the time he originated the statement in Philippians 4:13, "I can do all things through Christ who strengthens me."

This statement of faith was borne out of multiple hardships, not worldly success. It was quite an unusual setting for the call to victory that would eventually be embraced by athletes around the world. But before the athletes of today made this Bible verse well-known, prior to becoming a logo on the uniform for people of faith, long before it became approved as a fashion statement, there was a man who lived it in the spirit of Paul.

Chucky Mullins spent the final eighteen months of life on earth in a prison of his own. He was not detained by iron walls or the limits of a governing authority. Rather, he was trapped within his own motionless body.

It was the strength of Christ living inside the Apostle Paul that inspired him not only to endure but thrive in extreme circumstances. It seems that Chucky had an uncanny understanding and practice of this principle of faith that was introduced by Paul. When Chucky was asked what kept him going he would respond in this manner, "Carver and I read the Bible together, and he has not left my side during this whole time. This injury has really brought our family closer together."

Although Chucky knew he would never play football again, he had new dreams and goals: walk again, get a degree, coach football. Chucky would *Never Quit* believing, and he kept fighting through the toughest of times. When Chucky was asked for more specific details about his Bible reading with Carver, he shared his favorite verse, "I can do all things through Christ who strengthens me."

The football cleats have been removed, and one of the wristbands is missing. The uniform is now disheveled as I approach my youngest son on the playing field. I muster up my best effort to console him through his injury that has ended so many playing careers. He still has the Phil 4:13 eye-black in place because that's what the big boys do. But before the big boys wore it, two giants of faith and courage lived it.

24: ATTITUDE

IT IS THE DREAM OF MOST YOUNG BOYS GROWING UP IN THE STATE of Alabama to one day play football for their flagship university. For an outsider, it is hard to grasp the concept of the sanctity given to football for the University of Alabama. Having once lived in this state, I gained an understanding of how powerful the pull is for football but not just any football: Crimson Tide football. The hallowed grounds of Bryant-Denny Stadium are revered as a sanctuary to many. The truly faithful drape themselves in crimson attire like a religious vestment throughout the fall of each year. In this part of the Bible Belt there is only one day more sacred than Saturday, and for some it's a close competition. Alabama fans take to calling themselves *we* anytime a discussion arises about *their* football team. It seems that the label *we* is used most by those who never attended the University. Like a Christian who has never been to the Holy Land, it is not less holy to them. They are Alabama fans by choice, and many would say by the grace of God.

Chucky caught the fever and grew up wanting to play football for the University of Alabama. But there are only a select few who make it to Tuscaloosa and have the honor of representing this storied football program. They showed interest in him, but in the end, Chucky was not one of the chosen. Like a young teenager, he felt the flirtatious rejection of his first love.

Football is filled with the kind of disappointment that Chucky felt at not being selected. At times it seems that football takes much more than it gives, says *no* more than *yes*. I have a love-hate relationship with the game. My journey was similar to Chucky's—not being a highly recruited athlete out of high school. These raw emotions ran deep as I watched my son play his first little league football game. The sport had taken from Chucky, it had taken from me, and now it appeared that it was about to take from my youngest son after his very first game.

Luke's first football game started with much promise for my chances as a proud papa. He was excited about competing as a rookie in the ten-and-eleven-year-old league. As a young ten year old, he was one of the smaller players on the field. Despite his size, or lack thereof, the coaches inserted him at middle linebacker when he entered the game on defense.

His first play from scrimmage evolved as if it was choreographed by fate. The biggest, strongest, and fastest player in the league was on the opposing line of scrimmage. The ball was snapped and given to this bruiser who looked like a man among boys. Of course he headed right for Luke as the die of the meeting had been cast. It was a combination of events that took place next. Between moving to the ball, getting in the way, and getting run over, Luke was in the right place at the right time, or the wrong place at the wrong time. In either case, Luke grabbed hold of this raging beast as he burst through the hole, like he was in a rodeo bullpen. He somehow held on as the young bull began to decelerate under the added weight of Luke's cumbersome fifty pounds. He stumbled and Luke reached for a tighter hold around the now-fragile legs. He went down in a sudden burst that must have felt like felling a mighty oak to Luke's lean body.

I would like to say that Luke went on to prominence and made every tackle the rest of the scrimmage. But the bruiser took umbrage from Luke's bulldogging abilities. On each play after that, if the bruiser didn't receive the ball, he would hunt down Luke for a bone-crushing block. Luke ended most of the plays on his backside, led by his head and shoulders. Each time he was knocked down, it would take him a little longer to get up and waddle back to the huddle.

Mercifully, the game ended, and Luke came walking in my direction with his head down in exhaustion. As he arrived at the safety of his daddy's side, away from the gaze and potential heckling of his teammates, he removed his helmet. His hair was soaked with sweat, and he shook his head before uttering his resignation. Luke was about to retire from football after his first official contest, and I couldn't really blame him. This is the injury I spoke of earlier that has ended many football futures: a bruised and broken spirit from getting knocked down too many times by the hard hits of the game. It is the emotional wound that sometimes surpasses the physical pummeling and can take away the desire to continue participating in the sport.

He looked around to check that no one was watching or within earshot prior to making his prepared statement. Raising his eyes to mine, ensuring that he had my full attention, he asked, "Dad, did you see me tackle that big boy?"

Luke had arrived at a crossroads decision about his head-banging escapade. Similar choices have to be made on a daily basis by adults who compete in the game called life. Do we dwell most upon the knock-downs in life, or do we focus on the times we stand in the hole, hold on for dear life, and tackle the opponent?

The manner in which we respond to adversity is directly related to our *attitude*. A positive approach or good attitude doesn't mean we ignore our failures as if they didn't happen. Rather, we choose to celebrate our victories more than wallowing in the defeats. A winning *attitude* will prevent us from being conquered by the losses in life.

Chucky could have gotten wrapped up in the *why* of his circumstances when Alabama did not offer him a scholarship. But he chose not to be consumed with *why* Alabama said *no*. Instead he focused his attention upon getting Ole Miss to say *yes*.

From Chucky's viewpoint, the Rebels represented the next-best fit for him to play football in the SEC. When Ole Miss took a glance at him, he set his sights firmly upon them.

Head Football Coach Billy Brewer welcomed Chucky into his office on the weekend of his official visit to Ole Miss. Coach Brewer began the conversation with pieces of the rejection statement that he had shared so many times before: "Chucky, I like you. You have a great attitude, son, but sometimes that is not enough. You are not fast enough, big enough, or good enough to play in this league. You will fit in well at the Division II level but not in the SEC."

Chucky countered, "Coach, I promise you I can play here. Just give me a chance and you will never regret it." He said this looking straight into the eyes of the head football coach. Eyes sharp, smile wide, heart pleading, *your move coach.*

The smile had become contagious now as the gritty coach shot one back in Chucky's direction, saying "We are supposed to be selling you on our football program, and you have been selling me instead."

But just as suddenly as the smile crossed the coach's face, his expression now turned serious, almost somber. "I'm not gonna offer you a scholarship. The best I can do is to keep you in mind if one of the other kids backs out of his commitment to come here."

Years later, Brewer reflected upon that office visit with the precision of an event that has passed only moments earlier. "Someone did back out of his commitment, and we had to fill the spot. One of my assistants said, 'I vote for Chucky Mullins because he is your kind of player, Coach.'"

Billy Brewer's eyes glistened with emotion as he expressed what sold him on Chucky Mullins. "It was his *attitude.* He never looked back at Alabama. He could not have been happier, that was his *attitude. 'I'm an SEC football player.'*" Like so many other recipients of Chucky's charisma, the coach was changed for life. "He came to Ole Miss for a reason..."

Coach Brewer is not the first in his profession to be wooed by the *attitude* of one of his soldiers. Any coach will tell you that a player's *attitude* is central to his performance on the field of play.

The effects of a good *attitude* are not a modern-day gateway to success. The importance of, and appreciation for, a good *attitude* was stated in the prison letter of Paul. He gave up a high position of respect in the Jewish Church. His prior role as a prominent persecutor of the early Christians would have inspired a tendency toward pride. Yet he pressed upon his friends of the new faith to be filled with humility rather than pride. He encouraged them to take on the humility of the One he served: Jesus.

Humility is a funny thing. I have been instructed to be careful about praying for humility because you might get *humbled*. We don't become humble by working harder, but we work harder because we are humble. Paul understood that one's capacity to be humble hinged upon a person's attitude. His own words while being held prisoner in Rome are, "Your *attitude* should be the same as that of Christ Jesus...who humbled himself." (Phil 2:5)

Chucky, in the spirit of Paul, did not see rejection as defeat. Chucky was overlooked by the home school; Paul was thrown out of his home church. Chucky was knocked down when Alabama said that it didn't have a spot for him. But he also displayed a spirit similar to that of my son, Luke, playing in his first football game. Chucky held on for dear life, for the small glimmer of opportunity given by Ole Miss. He tugged and pulled until he brought down the improbable giant of playing football in the SEC.

Luke asked me, hungry for approval, "Dad, did you see me tackle that big boy?"

Chucky offered his satisfaction with a smile and the attitude best captured by Coach Brewer. "His attitude was, *Hey I'm playing football in the SEC. I couldn't have it any better.* Man, I loved that kid."

25: LOVE

HE WAS JUST A FRESHMAN PLAYING IN A FOOTBALL GAME FOR OLE Miss. Late in the game, he made a crushing tackle against an opposing receiver. He would later remember that the hit hurt him an *"awful lot."* A few minutes after the collision, he blacked out. He threw up several times over the weekend and was plagued with excruciating headaches. These are signs of a concussion, an injury that would require a modern player to be sidelined for an extended period. But the following Monday he was on the field again, as if the nightmare hit had only been a dream. "I didn't tell anyone that I had been hurt because I was afraid I would be cut from the team." Football was his best hope for escaping poverty and making it in life. Besides that, he loved the game too much and would not let someone else dictate his participation.

This tale sounds familiar to anyone who's heard of Chucky Mullins, but it's not his story. This is a glimpse into the life of his college football coach, Billy "Dog" Brewer. This one hit was similar to the injury that would affect Chucky Mullins. Both happened in an instant, and both would plague the coach for the rest of his life.

Brewer was given the nickname "Dog" as a player for the Rebels, and it aptly defined his approach to the game. He had the tenacity of a small cur that attacks any challenger venturing into its backyard.

"He was undersized, but boy he would hit you," said Warner

Alford, a teammate of the Dog and athletic director throughout Brewer's tenure as head coach at Ole Miss.

He approached his coaching career with the same pit-bull mentality. Langston Rogers was the University's longtime sports information director and remembered him this way, "Billy was always at his best when his back was against a wall. Some of his biggest seasons were when we were picked to finish last." True to his name, you didn't want to back the Dog into a corner. He was an old-school coach who could get in a player's face without pushing too hard. He had fought for everything he had gotten in life and wanted the same for his players. He was successful at the high school coaching ranks and in all of his collegiate assignments. At each stop, his first year on the job, he turned perennial losers into a winning team.

Brewer also had a keen affection for the creature from which his nickname derived. It's not clear if he got his name because he liked dogs so much or if he liked dogs so much because of his name— perhaps a little of both. He always had his trusted Labrador retriever, "Gee Bee," with him at practice. The tail-wagger was immensely loyal and hungry for Brewer's affection. At one practice, Gee Bee climbed the steep ladder to the coaches' tower in an effort to get to his master. It was an anomaly for the players, who were accustomed to Brewer's no-nonsense motivation, to see him so gentle with his trusted friend.

If Brewer's unorthodox act of allowing his dog on the practice field was a problem for anyone, they never said so. This may be attributed to the fact that no one would have dared question the "Big Dog" on his turf. That was his territory, and he managed it with the diplomacy of a junkyard dog. He was in charge of that backyard, and everyone knew it.

But the truth is, Gee Bee was not a hindrance to practice; in fact, everybody liked him. Good dogs have a profound effect upon people. They are loved by all, and people are glad to be in their presence. Gee Bee reciprocated the behavior of his two-legged friends by loving everyone he met. There seemed to be a connection to Gee Bee's willingness to love and the way he inspired others to love him. Could the same truth exist for us human animals as well? Surely the more we love others, the more they will love us in return.

Gee Bee wasn't the only extended family member for which Brewer had a special affection. Even today, he still speaks of Chucky as if he were his own son. Sure, his love for Chucky was rooted on a personal level. He saw much of his own story that reminded him of Chucky's. But I suspect that there was another monumental reason behind Brewer's warmth for this special kid. Chucky had mastered the same secret to a person's heart that Gee Bee had perfected, leaving Brewer defenseless against Chucky's nurturing spirit. Chucky loved everybody, so how could you not *love* him?

I asked Langston Rogers how he thought Coach Brewer was able to take Ole Miss to a bowl game in his first season, since the Rebels had five losing seasons in a row prior to his arrival. "I think it was his *love* for Ole Miss."

Perhaps his players sensed this *love* for them as well, and knew he would fight for them and their university. He loved the game, loved Ole Miss, and loved Chucky Mullins. *Love* is a powerful thing. It helped Billy Brewer turn losers into winners, and helped Chucky Mullins win the heart of his old-school coach.

26: RACE

IT'S A SIMPLE PHOTO OF TWO HANDS, ONE TOUCHING THE OTHER. The hand on top has a fair-colored skin tone and is weather-beaten. The hand underneath is a shade of dark brown with a fragile and unused appearance.

The photo is a prized possession of former Ole Miss Head Football Coach Billy Brewer. It's a glimpse of an intimate moment shared by him and Chucky Mullins in August 1990. The shot was taken on the day Chucky returned to Oxford, Mississippi, to resume his education—ten months after his injury.

A filmmaker recently asked Brewer to talk about race relations at Ole Miss. This is a sensitive subject for the man who grew up the best friend of black kids in Columbus, Mississippi. From there, he went to Ole Miss and was a part of the all-white football team in the late 1950s.

In response to the question, Brewer walks across the room of his home and retrieves the photo displaying two different hands. It has been said that a picture can say a thousand words. But Brewer does not need that many syllables to express what the photo says to him. He displays a tattered copy of the picture from 25 years prior.

"Yes, we have a tainted past, but this is how I see race." Brewer's grasp of Chucky's hand is symbolic of the way Chucky Mullins touched so many lives without moving a muscle. It is obvious that the old coach is one of those affected by his former player. Eyes glistening, he points to the photo and whispers. "To me...this picture says it all."

In the fall of 1962, James Meredith arrived to an unwelcoming greeting at the University of Mississippi. He bravely approached the steps of the historic Lyceum building escorted by armed military. He would be the first African-American student admitted to the University amidst intense objection and rioting that left two people dead.

In the fall of 1973, Ben Williams and James Reed became the first African-American players for the Ole Miss Rebels football team. Reed was an excellent student athlete, and Williams was an unequaled talent on the football field. Ben Williams was affectionately given the name *Gentle Ben* as he won the hearts of his fellow classmates of a differing *race*. In the process, he became the first African-American to be elected by the student body as Colonial Reb, the title given each year to a student chosen to be Mr. Ole Miss.

Coach Brewer utilizes the photo as an example of how the Ole Miss journey with *race* has been complicated. Throughout its history, Ole Miss has been recognized for the visible shortcomings that have accompanied its path to equality. This makes it easy to overlook the progress that has been lovingly interwoven by many along the way.

One of these individuals who made a difference was Deano Orr who came to campus in the fall of 1989. He was the salutatorian of his high school graduating class in Courtland, Alabama. He would become a four-year letterman on the Ole Miss Rebels football team. With their hometowns just forty miles apart, he also became a traveling companion and dear friend to Chucky Mullins.

Orr has worked 20 years for one of the world's largest paper and forest products companies. Today he is the executive director of the corporation's charitable foundation and global giving programs. The focus of his efforts for the organization is to provide environmental education and literacy improvements throughout the world.

He is also a member of the University of Mississippi's alumni board where he sits on the executive committee. He speaks of his alma mater with love and pride, saying, "I view Ole Miss as a university of reconciliation. It started with the two men—James Meredith and Ben Williams—who broke down the walls for African-Americans like myself."

Deano Orr has a deep respect and appreciation for Head Coach Billy Brewer and for former teammate Chucky Mullins. He believes that these two men took up tools to build upon the groundwork laid by Meredith and Williams. He explains, "Chucky Mullins and Billy Brewer are integral parts of how far we have come as people, a school, and a family. Their tandem efforts had a profound effect upon *race* relations at the University."

In the early eighties, an African-American player once told Brewer, "Coach, I think you have a black soul." Orr saw this same spirit as he witnessed Brewer laying the track for unification on the 1989 Rebels team.

"I will never forget our first week on campus for two-a-day practices. Coach Brewer told us to wear our best clothes on Sunday because we were going to church." Deano says this with a smile because his faith has always been central to his life.

"Sure enough, he loaded up over thirty of us freshman and took us to an African-American church for worship. The next week he gave us the same message. This time the destination was *his* church filled with all white faces."

The third week he told them to go to the church of their choice but encouraged them to go somewhere. The two weeks of team church was certainly a celebration of faith. But it was something else as well…a commitment by Brewer to continually erode the barriers of separation.

For his part in race relations, Chucky's warmth and love for others was infectious. After the injury, Orr remembers how Chucky always had a mob of people around him on campus that transcended *race*. The Ole Miss community saw him not for the color of his skin, but as a person that they wanted to emulate. "I recall the next game after Chucky's injury as a day of healing. Fans throughout Vaught-Hemmingway Stadium, regardless of *race* and socio-economic status, came together in one accord to assist a young man who was fighting for his life. That marked a monumental day in Ole Miss history."

Deano also explained the unity his teammate inspired. "Chucky's injury not only disarmed racism but helped the Ole Miss Family come together for a common cause. But his ability to bring fans and students together extended far beyond the confines of Vaught-Hemingway Stadium. Throughout the South, and at other SEC schools, people from all backgrounds worked in harmony to collect funds to support Chucky. Chucky always had a way of bringing people together."

Chucky Mullins and Billy Brewer walked us down the road of progress at Ole Miss. However, the University, like all broken people, still is a work in process. We have yet to arrive, but Ole Miss is gaining ground as a result of Chucky's gifts of courage, respect and reconciliation.

In early 2014, two freshmen defamed the statue of James Meredith erected on the Ole Miss campus. In response, Chancellor Dan Jones invited some local alumni and community leaders to work together for brighter days, while still in the shade of this dark event. One of the first invitees to that important gathering was Deano Orr.

This action speaks of the chancellor's commitment to lead Ole Miss into a model for advancement in relationships. It is also a salute to the ambassadorship that Deano Orr has always expressed. "I truly love Ole Miss and am proud to be a part of the Ole Miss family."

When Billy Brewer grasped Chucky Mullins hand that day in

Oxford, his gesture communicated something beyond words. His gentle expression conveyed to Chucky: *We're gonna finish this RACE together.* The player and coach were united in their commitment to overcome the shackles of paralysis. They also shared a zeal to conquer the barriers that separate us from sharing love in a manner that transcends *race*.

It seems that Billy Brewer and Chucky Mullins were not the last black and white team committed to joining forces to eclipse hurdles at Ole Miss. Dan Jones and Deano Orr have picked up the baton and continue with the *race* to reconciliation.

Even today, Deano Orr speaks of the lasting impact his teammate had upon him. "I strive to personally exemplify the courage and tenacity of Chucky. His spirit will always live on within me."

Because of Rebels like Billy Brewer, Dan Jones, and Deano Orr, the spirit of Chucky Mullins will continue to move us forward until the *race* is finally won.

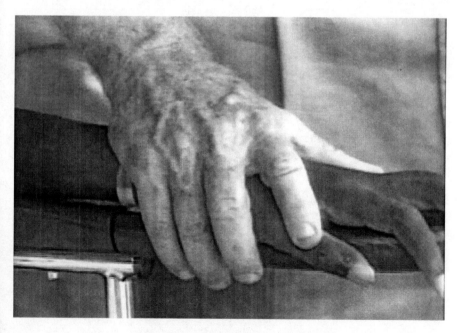

Coach Billy Brewer embracing Chucky

27: FRIEND

"MR. WILLIAMS, CAN YOU CUT MY HAIR TODAY?" THE HIGH SCHOOL
student knew the answer before he asked the question. Special education teacher Sebastian Williams always cut his hair, along with several
of his classmates' hair.

"Yeah, come by after you finish lunch, and I will hook you
up, little brother," Mr. Williams replied. He was a fine mentor
to young men, and another gift he shared with them was a fresh
haircut. He had the skill to sculpture their crown with the precision and flare of a well-compensated practitioner of his craft. But
Mr. Williams did not perform the work of art to get paid. Instead, he was depositing an emotional investment into the lives of
these young men. He helped them to feel more confident about
themselves by their renewed appearance. In the process, he communicated how much he valued his pupils by performing this
task for free.

Before his days as an educator, Sebastian "Snake" Williams was a
rookie on the 1988 Ole Miss Football team along with Chucky Mullins. He can recite effortlessly from memory the details of the first head
of hair that he ever cut.

"Snake, get up and cut my hair!" Chucky Mullins barked as he
barged into the room of his new friend.

"Man, I don't know how to cut hair," Snake protested.

"It's a bald head; all you gotta do is take it off," Chucky said, pressing on right through Snake's roadblock. He possessed an uncanny charisma that encouraged others to action.

Chucky's logic won out, and Snake postured himself behind a chair, draped a towel over Chucky's shoulders, and proceeded to give his first official haircut.

Just as Snake was gaining the sea-legs of his trimming technique, other teammates walked by the room and proclaimed in unison: "Snake, I didn't know you could cut hair!"

Before Snake could wearily explain that these were waters he had never treaded before, Chucky intervened, saying, "Yep, he's good at it, too!"

Jealous and eager to look their best, the others jumped in line. "All right, dude, I'm next after you finish with Chucky."

Before you can learn to cut hair, or accomplish anything in life, someone has to give you a chance. Sometimes, when another believes in you, it helps you to believe in yourself. Or in the words of Snake himself, "I didn't know I could cut hair until Chucky told me that I could." This maiden voyage with the clippers helped them to set sail on a great *friend*-ship from that day forward. Chucky sprinkled a little confidence on Snake that day. Since then, Snake has been using his skill to pour confidence into others—by helping them to look and be their best.

While Snake and Chucky became fast friends, his teammate, Scott "Swat" Swatzell, was having a hard time adjusting to his new roommate after a couple of weeks on campus. There are certain people we just don't connect with. It presents an extra challenge when we are forced to share a room with that person in a strange new place.

Swat's roommate never missed a party or opportunity to go out on the town. He was more motivated to enjoy college life than to participate in football or academics. The free-spirited bunkmate would only make it one semester on the team. Looking back now, Swat reflects that his roommate didn't really have a *friend* on the team, except for Chucky. Swat remembers Chucky this way, "The way he would befriend a person…Didn't matter if you were black, white, green, rich, poor, scholarship athlete, walk-on athlete, he just wanted to be your *friend*."

Unlike his roommate, Swat was extremely driven about his academics, as well as athletics, and eventually attained a master's in engineering. He hit the books right after dinner each night and would rarely go out or even down the hall to play video games. Swat remembers Chucky's romps into his room. "About every other day, Chucky would drop by my room, see me studying and immediately pounce on my bed like Tigger (from Winnie the Pooh)—doing everything he could to divert my attention from schoolwork, messing up my bed and the like. He would nearly cave my bed in laughing and shouting. You couldn't help but laugh. I look back at these times now and truly believe God was using Chucky to help impart some levity into my life. Provide some relief in the stress."

Chucky met needs for both Snake and Swat by being a *friend*. He gave to Snake by making him feel *more* important. He gave to Swat by allowing him to feel *less* important. That's what friends do—they accept us as we are and help transform us into something more.

Derrick King from Pontotoc, Mississippi, was Chucky's roommate our first year on campus. He shares how Chucky loved his music. "There was a song titled *Let's Chill* that was made popular by a group named *Guy*. Chucky would sing that song all the time, and when we were in the room he played it all the time," King reminisces with a laugh.

A portion of the lyrics contained this appeal: "Let's chill and let's settle down." The lyrics were about a man trying to woo a woman toward his affection. But Chucky would often apply it when *friends* were getting heated in a discussion. He would bust out singing in the midst of a tense altercation, "Let's chill and let's settle down."

King remembers, "It was a love song, and that's who Chucky was, a person of love for everyone." He transformed the song to speak for love and *friend*ship between all.

Snake Williams cuts the hair of his students to meet their needs. But I suspect that a portion of this gesture meets a need for him as well. It is his way of celebrating the memory of his *friend* who taught him how to cut hair without ever lifting the razor himself. Chucky had a similar impact upon people after his injury. He continued to teach others to live with a commitment to friendship, love, and reconciliation, all without lifting a finger. It was his affection for others that drew him to the song "Let's Chill." And it was this warmth that stirred in others a desire to be his *friend*.

Chucky having fun with Keshia

28: TOUGH

IT'S 1987, THE FUTURE OLE MISS REBEL WAS PLAYING IN HIS LAST football game as a high-school competitor. This was an All-Star event, in which the best players in the state had been selected to showcase their talents. His opportunity to stand out came when a pass was thrown to a receiver, right in front of his safety position. He drove his body into the offender headfirst, and recorded a bone-crushing tackle. He sustained a concussion on the play, and it would be an hour later before he would regain coherence.

He brought this same aggressive style of play to the college game when he joined the Rebels later that fall. Although he was not one of the larger players on the team, there was none any tougher to suit-up for the Red and Blue. He would tear into the biggest player on the team and exchange blows if he felt he had been disrespected. He was one of those guys you just didn't want to mess with. You might win the battle, but the next play, the next series, the next practice, he would be back for more.

It's the fall of 2008 in Ann Arbor, Michigan, and the tough guy has traded in his Rebels' helmet for a Wolverines' whistle. He is in his seventeenth year of coaching and first as the linebackers coach for the University of Michigan. On the first day of fall practice the freshmen receive the remarks that the varsity had already gotten in the prior spring practice. "Guys, the first thing we are going to learn is the proper way to tackle. I know you guys can 'hit' because you're linebackers. I am not concerned with how hard you hit, but how well you tackle, and that you're doing it the proper way."

As the tackling drill begins, the freshmen are confused by a strange new language. There was one word in particular they had never heard before. The interpretation was complicated because the utterance was pronounced with a Southern accent: "Buuu-ya-nay-uck!" The passionate directive was actually three words, not one, but they held one central meaning for the coach.

Many who reside from below the Mason-Dixon Line have this special ability of vocal resonation. Condensing several words into what sounds like a single harmonious comment, with multiple syllables. Here is an example: "doin-ah-ite." Properly translated, this single utterance is communicating a five-word question: "Are you doing all right?"

Mercifully, an upper classman finally gave in and assisted the freshmen with understanding the repetitive cry of "Buuu-ya-nay-uck!" by this coach from Mississippi. "He's telling you to 'bull-your-neck' when you make a tackle."

Finally the coach stops the drill and moves into a dramatization as he acts out the precise movement that he is looking for. "You lead with your head up, never down. Engage the opponent with your head on a forty-five degree angle. Contact is made with your forehead, or top of your facemask, never the crown or top of your head." They finally understood the mantra of "bull-your-neck"—come at the opponent like a charging bull—eyes on the target and head up.

One newcomer muttered under his breath, "I can't bring it like that."

The senior starter was unimpressed by the rookie and simplified things by saying, "Well you ain't goin' to play, then. Hop is serious about that. He played with this dude who broke his neck."

The "dude" was Chucky Mullins and "Coach Hop" was Chucky's teammate, Jay Hopson. The player who embodied *toughness* while at Ole Miss was teaching his young players another attribute. Not only did he want his players to exert themselves with tough play, but more importantly, smart play.

In 2012, Hopson brought his *toughness* home to Mississippi when he became the head football coach at Alcorn State University in Lorman. Alcorn State participates in the Southwestern Athletic Conference, a league made up of historically black colleges and universities. The school is best known as the alma mater of former NFL greats Steve McNair and Donald Driver. But the school attained new fame when it hired Hopson, who became the first white head coach to represent any school in their conference.

Pittsburgh Steelers legend Rocky Bleier once described *toughness* with these words: "*Toughness* is doing the things you *don't* want to do with the same enthusiasm as the things that you *do* want to do." Jay Hopson would need this type of *toughness* to fight on past the naysayers as he took over the reins at Alcorn State. Some were not happy with the thought of this white guy running their football program. The only thing he wanted to do was coach football, but he embraced the challenges of his position with the enthusiasm of Rocky Bleier. Eventually his *toughness* won the hearts and minds of the home team. In 2013, he led the Braves to a five-win improvement over 2012, resulting in a 9-3 record. In addition, he became a finalist for the Eddie Robinson FCS Coach of the Year Award (FCS is an abbreviation for the NCAA Division I Football Championship Subdivision).

Chucky Mullins brought the same brand of toughness to football as his teammate Jay Hopson. Chucky was relentless in his courage for attacking bigger players head-first. Teammate Snake Williams remembers, "Chucky had scars all over the top of his helmet from where he would slam into a tackle."

This was much the culture for those of us who played in this era of football. Always tackling head-first, inflicting as much damage as we could into the opponent, and accepting whatever injuries we might incur as an occupational hazard. We, like many before us, did not fully appreciate the permanence of concussions, neck injuries or paralysis.

By the time Jay Hopson arrived to coach at Michigan, he was defining *toughness* differently from how he had in his youth. As practice ended that fall day in 2008, Hopson had one final pep talk for his young Wolverines. "Look, I know you guys think it looks *tough* when you drive a man back into the ground, leading with the top of your head. I know. I've done it."

The players are tired, sweating, and breathing hard. But Hopson still has their attention with his deep, tough-guy voice—like Rocky Balboa with a Southern accent. "I been knocked out four or five times tackling that way. I learned the hard way, that's not *tough*. Let me tell you what is *tough*. It's sitting by the bed of your teammate who can't move below his neck because he used to tackle that way, too. *Tough* is reaching over to that friend with a little hand-held vacuum and sucking the mucus out of the hole in his neck just so he can breathe. Guys, believe me, that's *tough*."

I, too, view *toughness* in a new way these days. Chucky displayed *toughness* by putting his head into the action while on the field of play. But perhaps his greatest display of *toughness* was the way he responded to his injury with such grace. His attitude in the light of tragedy has inspired in others a refusal that he be forgotten. And because we don't forget him, we remember how he impacted the game forever. I think Rocky Bleier would believe Chucky met his description of *toughness*. Like his teammate Jay Hopson, all Chucky ever wanted to do was play and coach football. He never wanted to be injured, but he accepted what was placed upon him with the same enthusiasm that he took to the field. He has become for many a true definition of what it means to be *tough*.

29: REASON

IN THE FALL OF 1989, I WAS ON TOP OF THE WORLD—AS A FRESH-
man, I was on the Ole Miss Rebels football team. I had made the
travel squad by securing a spot on the kick-return team and would
be playing in the SEC. But just one week before our first game I
came crashing back to earth when I tore the cartilage in my right
knee. My hopes of lettering as a freshman were crushed by an un-
timely injury that sidelined me from the playing field.

I searched to find *reason* in the hand dealt to me by cruel fate.
I was depressed and frustrated by the injury. Like a game lost at
the last second, I was emotionally distraught to be put out of play
before the game even started. But just two months later, I received
a big dose of reality, ending my pity party, when my friend Chucky
Mullins suffered a much more serious injury.

After I got hurt, Chucky became my replacement on the
kick-return team. I considered the possibility that my injury could
have played a role in Chucky's accident, and I was plagued with
troubling questions: *Had his performance on the kick-return team
improved Chucky's confidence and enhanced his playing time as a pass
defender? If I had not hurt my knee, would he have been on the field
when the injury occurred against Vanderbilt?*

I am not the first person who has been personally affected by a
tragedy to ask questions like this. Some people find meaning in the
bad things of life by believing that *everything happens for a reason.*

Others find peace in believing that some things *just happen* for no apparent *reason* at all.

In searching for answers, perhaps the most helpful question is not: "Does everything happen for a *reason?*" Instead, a more helpful question might be: "Can we make *reason* out of everything that happens?"

The former question focuses on our *emotions* in response to peril, while the latter focuses on our *actions* in response to the same event. The first question concentrates on *why* an event happened, which we frequently can't control; the other emphasizes what we can control—our reaction to that event.

In our efforts to understand life-changing events, the most important thing to remember is not what we can do, but what God can do. There is a popular scripture found in Romans 8:28, and a portion of it says that *God works for good in everything.* I find it comforting to know that God is working to bring about good even in the midst of bad. I am also grateful for what the text doesn't proclaim: this teaching doesn't say everything that happens is *good* in God's eyes. Neither does it say that God does *every*thing. We live in a broken world—there is pain, there are accidents, and there are questions. I do believe God is present in each circumstance but not as an orchestrator of bad. Instead, I view God more as a comforter and conqueror, creating good from the worst events in our lives.

Coach Billy Brewer believes that Chucky did not come to Ole Miss to get hurt but for a greater purpose. Brewer explains his feelings in this way, "He was an unusual person that God put on this earth. I think He put Chucky at Ole Miss for a *reason.*" I suspect that Coach Brewer is right—that Chucky came to Ole Miss for a *reason*—although we can't know on this side of heaven. But one thing is evident in our world today. Chucky brought sense and *reason* to the presumed senselessness of his traumatic injury. He continued to live his life with purpose, even after the injury. I believe, with the help of God, Chucky found the "good" in his tragedy.

And there is one other truth that I am sure of—Chucky influenced my desire to work for good in whatever bad may occur in my life. It was this hunger to make meaning out of life that inspired me to become a minister. Because Chucky showed me the way, I try to make *reason* out of everything that happens.

30: CHARITY

ON MONDAY, NOVEMBER 13, 1989, TWO WEEKS HAD PASSED SINCE
Chucky's injury. I rushed through my lunch in the dining hall of
the Kinard Hall Athletic Dormitory. I was scheduled to be dressed
and in the film room by 1:15 p.m. for a full afternoon of football
practice. Participation in college athletics comes with a demanding
lifestyle, and I had learned to treat every moment of free time as a
precious commodity. If I made good use of my time, I would have
exactly ten minutes to lie down and take a quick nap before departing for the Field House.

With the meal finished and nap completed, I drove to the practice facility. As I did each day, I navigated my car down fraternity
row. I passed the Sigma Nu fraternity house and saw two guys toss-
ing a football on the front lawn. I was envious of their seemingly
carefree afternoon and jealous of the freedom they had to enjoy
college life. I muttered to myself: *Those guys have no idea how good
they have it.*

As the two frat brothers tossed the ball to one another they rem-
inisced about their days on the football field. They knew that the
University had once hosted a full-contact fraternity football game.
These two former warriors of the gridiron flirted with the idea of
seeking the game's renaissance. They attended Ole Miss Rebels
games each week and thought of us college football players: *Those
guys have no idea how good they have it.*

As Bill Courtney caught the ball in front of the Sigma Nu house, his mind was on deeper matters. "Did you see the article in the back of the Daily Mississippian today?" Bill asked his fraternity brother and fellow pigskin fan John Quaka. "The article was about a high school kid named Allen Moore in Lauderdale, Mississippi. He had a football injury just like Chucky Mullins."

Bill had been a standout receiver for Auburndale High School in Memphis and caught the pass effortlessly as the conversation intensified. "What if we host a football game against another fraternity and give the money to this kid in Chucky's honor?"

John liked the idea of putting on the helmet and pads again. The thought that they could participate in such an event on behalf of others magnified his interest. "That would be awesome! Do you think you could pull it off?" Bill was the vice president of the fraternity, and John was deferring to his leadership skills to make it happen.

It had been well-documented that Chucky Mullins was responding to his injury with a staggeringly positive outlook, and Bill was inspired. "From what I hear, Chucky is a great guy, and I bet it would thrill him to help out someone else from the platform he's been placed upon."

John thought his friend had a good idea, but he was unaware that Bill had already committed to turning this *idea* into a *reality*. "Yes! It will take some work, but I have the contacts on campus to pull it together," Bill answered without hesitation.

With John's encouragement, Bill was eager to find out more about the young man from Lauderdale, Mississippi. Bill phoned Allen Moore's high school coach and was given more details. He learned that the only financial support for Allen's injury was a $15,000 medical policy. The coach had shared that the injury was horrific, and he did not know if he could continue coaching the sport. "They don't even have assistance to buy a wheel chair," the coach said sorrowfully, as he poured his heart out to Bill.

In the spring of 1990, the Sigma Nu fraternity played against Phi Delta Theta in what was dubbed the "Charity Bowl." The combined efforts of the two fraternities raised a total of $16,000. At halftime in the contest, Ole Miss Head Football coach Billy Brewer and Bill Courtney of Sigma Nu fraternity presented a check to Allen Moore in honor of Chucky Mullins.

The game was such a success that they decided to have it again the next year. This time Sigma Nu doubled the proceeds from the prior year and assisted another victim of paralysis.

On March 21, 2014, the Sigma Nu Fraternity hosted its 25th consecutive Charity Bowl. The 25th recipient to be assisted was a young man named Stevelyn Robinson. He was presented with a check in the amount of $75,000. Since the bowl's inception, Sigma Nu has raised $1.4 million for victims of paralysis. It has become one of the largest collegiate philanthropies in the country.

Bill Courtney reflects upon the success of the Charity Bowl, saying, "As a Sigma Nu officer I did a lot on campus at Ole Miss, but I am most proud of starting the Charity Bowl. It has become one of my crowning achievements in life." This is not a trite statement when you consider the fullness with which Bill Courtney has impacted our world for good.

Many of us connected to football were tempted with the same struggles as Allen Moore's high school coach. *Unsure we could go on and still participate in a sport that could have such tragic consequences.* Some, however, like Bill Courtney, ran toward the challenges and pain of football while utilizing it to positively impact others.

Bill Courtney founded Classic American Hardwood in 2001. Today, the company is thriving with 120 employees being enriched by Bill's leadership. In 2003, Bill became a volunteer football coach at Memphis' inner city Manassas High School. He eventually became the head coach and transformed the perennial losing team into champions. These were amazing results for a part-time coach who ran a multi-million dollar business in his day job. So inspiring was his story that he became the focus of a Hollywood documentary titled "Undefeated." The production would go on to win the 2012 Academy Award for Best Feature Length Documentary.

"I am convinced that there would have never been a Charity Bowl had Chucky Mullins not responded to his injury with such grace." Bill Courtney explained this statement by acknowledging Chucky's character, resolve, and endearing disposition. "I also believe, with every ounce of faith inside of me, that Chucky Mullins was designed by God for that moment."

Those guys have no idea how good they have it. That was the perception I had of the Sigma Nu fraternity boys as I drove to practice that fall day in 1989. They held that same opinion of those of us fortunate enough to still be playing football. Through the inspiration of Chucky Mullins, we were both able to eventually see how good *we* had it. Instead of relishing what the other had, we celebrated our own fortunes. It is that attitude that inspires people to take on endeavors of *charity*. When we count our blessings, then and only then can we strive to be a blessing to the world around us.

The slogan of the Sigma Nu fraternity is made up of three words: Love, Honor, and Truth. *Charity* is another word for love in some translations of the Bible.

I am grateful that there are brave people like Bill Courtney who not only speak the creed of *charity* but also practice it with honor and truth. *Charity*: what a grand word for love. The Charity Bowl is indeed an abundant reflection of love and a worthy celebration of Chucky Mullins. But Bill Courtney, consistent with his character, credits another with its implementation. "It all started as a result of Chucky Mullins. He is the inspiration for us all."

31: COURAGE

DEREK JONES IS A FOOTBALL COACH. HE AND HIS FAMILY LIVE WITH the understanding that no move is permanent in his chosen line of work. Living with the temporary nature of this profession, there are some things that never seem to get unpacked when the Jones family moves to a new town.

Among the long-term storage items are the numerous trophies and accolades Derek Jones achieved as a standout track and football star for the Ole Miss Rebels. Like other family treasures, they remain in boxes. Perhaps when Derek eventually retires from the profession of football, the relics will reemerge. Maybe then he will have a trophy room to display the brass and wooden objects that honor the man he once was.

So it is no surprise when you walk into Coach Jones' office at Duke University that there is not an elaborate display of his accomplishments. He has served as an assistant coach for the Blue Devils football team since 2008. The lack of fanfare in his office speaks to the humility of the man.

But among the bare walls in his corner of the athletics complex resides the recognition of one accomplishment. The simple plaque has persevered through each coaching stop Derek has made in the collegiate ranks. Jones explains, "This is the one award that I have always displayed in every place that I have coached." For the uninformed it presents as many questions as answers. But these are questions that Jones is happy to answer as he glances at his name written in red on the wooden surface. The words at the top of the memento read: *Chucky Mullins Courage Award.*

Since 1990, a player has been chosen prior to each season who most embodies the spirit, *courage*, and attitude of Chucky Mullins. The honoree has the privilege of wearing number 38 on behalf of Chucky Mullins and is known as the "Chucky Mullins Courage Award" winner. Derek Jones was a four-year letterman for the Ole Miss Rebels from 1993-1996. He became the seventh recipient of the award.

Eventual NFL players Alundis Brice, Nate Wayne, Ronnie Heard, Patrick Willis, and Jamarca Sanford preceded their professional careers by receiving the "Chucky Mullins Courage Award." But perhaps no Rebel 38 has embodied the *courage* of the award more than the twenty-second recipient, Deterrian Shackelford. In March of 2011, he tore ligaments in his knee during the last week of spring practice and would miss the entire season. In spite of the injury, or perhaps in part because of how he responded, he was still chosen to represent the team as Number 38 for the 2011 season.

The next season he reinjured his knee and once again was sidelined. He had graduated in May of that year but would miss all of the 2012 season as well. Surely no one would have blamed him had he hung up the cleats for good after the second injury. In exchange for his degree, Deterrian had given the University two quality years of football while suffering through two years of rehabilitation. But after a two-year hiatus from the field of play, he competed for the Rebels as a graduate student in each game of the 2013 season.

In early 2014, Deterrian sought a sixth year of eligibility as a result of missing two complete seasons due to injury. For spring break 2014 he decided to forego beaches filled with white sands and beautiful girls. Still, the setting for his break from school offered plenty of heat, but the sights were of competitors running in his direction with a ball. He was back on the football field again.

But the football field where Shackelford found himself was what we Americans call a soccer field. He was not in Mississippi, or even the United States, but the third world country of Haiti. This is how Deterrian Shackelford chose to spend his spring break: in mission and service to people in need.

At home and abroad, Shackelford has become a champion for community service and charitable endeavors. At the end of spring football practice in 2014, Shackelford was once again elected to represent Number 38 for the Ole Miss Rebels. He is the first ever two-time recipient of the *Chucky Mullins Courage Award*. It seems that the Rebels coaches understand that one of the greatest displays of *courage* is when we give of ourselves for others.

"The impact that those two knee surgeries had on me, I kind of took on the spirit that Chucky displayed and brought it with me every day in the training room and with everything I did. I never knew I would have that kind of connection with him," Shackelford said after accepting the award on Saturday, April 5, 2014.

Chucky Mullins embraced life, and all of its challenges, with extreme *courage*. As a result, he threw down the gauntlet for future Rebel 38s like Derek Jones and Deterrian Shackelford to embody that same spirit.

Besides the *courage* award displayed in his Duke football office, Derek Jones has a single relic from his playing days displayed prominently in his home. It's his Number 38 jersey, framed. It inspires conversation about Chucky Mullins for all who see it. Jones explains, "I never knew Chucky, but you don't have to know a person to know what they were about. I tried to meet his approval when I wore 38, and to this day, I try to walk in the light of his *courage*."

Perhaps when he retires from the game of football Derek Jones will eventually have that trophy room to honor the player that he was. But for now he only displays one award to celebrate not only who he was but also who he is: a man forever changed by the *courage* of Chucky Mullins.

The second annual Chucky Mullins Courage Award presentation, pictured from left: Jeff Carter, Coach Billy Brewer, Chucky Mullins and Creek Mitchell

The first four Chucky Mullins Courage Award recipients, pictured from left: Trea Southerland, Johnny Dixon, Creek Mitchell and Jeff Carter

32 : CHOSEN

Jason Jones was *chosen* in 2012 to be the twenty-third recipient of the *Chucky Mullins Courage Award*. His dream is to one day play football in the NFL. But for now he is paying his dues with an indoor football team located in Denver, Colorado. Suspecting that he might be frustrated with the pace of his journey to the NFL, I asked Jason Jones in the spring of 2014 for an update. He responded like a natural-born man of courage, saying "It's going good and getting better!" It is with an attitude like this that Jason Jones truly embodies the character of Chucky Mullins.

Jones speaks with a healthy balance of pride about the selection process of becoming Number 38 for the Ole Miss Rebels. "It is a special honor because you have to be *chosen* to wear that number. You don't pick the number yourself."

He shared the following thoughts about his journey toward receiving the *Chucky Mullins Courage Award*, "I set my mind to earn the privilege of representing Chucky Mullins by wearing number 38. It has changed me and my family forever. I cherish the honor and strive to represent it with everything that I do."

In one breath, Jones speaks of being *chosen* to be 38, while in the next statement he hints at how the number was *chosen* by him. This seems to personify much of our success and failures in life. Some of what we become seems to be *chosen* for us, while a portion of who we are is *chosen* by us.

Jason Jones did not get to make the final decision if he would be *chosen* to represent Number 38. But he prepared himself for that opportunity when he made the choice to embrace the spirit of Chucky Mullins. He chose to embody all that Chucky Mullins stood for when he caught a glimpse of Chucky's integrity and passion for life.

I shared earlier how Chucky Mullins and his brother Horace made a choice to leave the home of Karen and Carver Phillips. After Chucky returned two weeks later, the Phillips never had an ounce of trouble out of Chucky. Horace made the choice not to return and by his 18th birthday had spent his first stint in jail.

In speaking with Horace's former guardian, Karen Phillips, and cousin, Dorothy Mullins, I envision him as a lovable soul. It seems that he is a good person who has made some bad choices.

Some believe that God *chose* Chucky for the purpose of leading Ole Miss into a more healthy existence as an institution of education and culture. While others view his injury as a tragic accident, that Chucky chose to give purpose. Perhaps the answer lies somewhere in the middle; as fleshed out by a fictitious football player from Alabama named Forrest Gump, "I don't know if we each have a destiny, or if we're all just floating around accidental-like on a breeze. But I...I think maybe it's both. Maybe both are happening at the same time."

I have a hard time believing that Chucky was *chosen* by God to be injured. One thing is certain, though, Chucky made the choice to respond to his injury with a grace that has forever changed our beloved Ole Miss.

In the University's press release regarding Jason Jones' selection as the *Chucky Mullins Courage Award* winner, he was described off the field in this way: "Jones is a psychology major and has made the SEC Academic Honor Roll. He has volunteered at the annual National Student-Athlete Day Community Service Project and the Special Olympics. He is a member of the Fellowship of Christian

Athletes leadership team and leads a Bible study group with his teammates. Jones also mentors local elementary school children and is an active member of the *Reading with the Rebels* program."

Jason Jones went a step further and embraced the family of Chucky Mullins with love of his own. The youngest member of the Carver and Karen Phillips family is their daughter, Aleshia. She is approaching her junior year of high school and describes Jones this way, "Jason became a brother to me, and I see Chucky through him every time I see him. Jason represented Chucky on the field and off the field. He helped his teammates during practice, games, and in the classroom."

I am grateful that the Ole Miss coaches chose a young man with the character of Jason Jones to represent Number 38. In the same breath, I give thanks that Jason has *chosen* to embody the spirit of Chucky in every walk of life. For me, the following statement speaks to the destiny of both Chucky Mullins and Jason Jones. He was *chosen* to be 38, and 38 was *chosen* by him.

33: WHY

"Why doesn't God give us a miracle?"

THAT IS THE QUESTION THAT MY WIFE, MONYA, AND I ASKED FRE-
quently when we learned of our son Noah's deafness in January of
1999. It was an especially cold and dark winter day when Noah was
diagnosed with profound bilateral sensorineural hearing loss at18
months old. Cold, I remember the numbness and empty feeling,
inside more so than outside, as we began phoning our family with
the words that our baby could not hear us say: "He's deaf." Darkness, rather than brightness, was the future outlook we saw on that
dreary day. "Why? Why? Why?" Realizing her words were nothing
more than a voiceless wind from her lips, Monya would plea, "I
just want my baby to hear me say *I love you*."

Moments turned into years living with Noah's deafness, but the
question remained. "Why can't I explain a Disney movie to my in-
quisitive little boy?" I would ask. But the most painful *whys* weren't
mine or even my wife's. It was the hollow-looking eyes of my son
when he wondered why none of his cousins had to wear hearing
aids or a cochlear implant. Yes, the most painful *why* of all came
from Noah himself when, after years of therapy, he could utter,
"Why...ears...broke?"

The questions that we asked were characteristic of a family facing grief and loss. I was in seminary, being educated as a minister,

when we received the diagnosis of Noah's deafness. I had the proper training about God and knew the right theology: *God doesn't make bad things happen—He conquers them.* I knew what to believe, as many of us do, until the peril hit too close to home. Then our theological house was not strong enough to endure the one question that plagues the faith of even the most spiritual among us: *Why?*

If there has ever been a person who earned the right to ask *why* it was Chucky Mullins. As a small child he had no father in his life and was raised in poverty by his mom and grandmother. Then life would offer more questions when death claimed both of these women before Chucky's thirteenth birthday. Finally, the paralysis took his best hope of overcoming the treacherous path that he had been given. Coach Billy Brewer is puzzled, even today, when contemplating Chucky's spiritual and emotional maturity, "He never, not once, ever said to me, 'Coach, why did this happen to me?'"

Chucky has inspired me to a new question: How did he not ask *why?*

It took years of healing for our young family, but we eventually stopped asking *why*. We replaced the *why* with *what*. Yes, Noah was deaf, and no, it was not fair. But how were our *whys* helping to make things better? We realized they were not. So the prevailing term became *what*. What can we do to help our son through this challenge? That is the question that helped usher us to the place of peace as a family – *what*.

We eventually arrived at that place of comfort together, with the support of professionals. This personal experience has propelled me to ponder even more the powerful reaction of Chucky Mullins. How could this twenty-year-old kid with no formal training, no elaborate support system, get beyond the *whys* of his life?

As with my own journey, I have stopped asking *why* when considering Chucky's amazingly positive attitude. I have refocused my concentration on *what* he did, not *why* he did it. He met the world with a smile, no matter what it chose to give him. He had a commitment to happiness that transcended circumstances.

The more I think about how Chucky responded to tragedy, the less I find myself asking *why* in my own circumstances. And the less I ask, the easier it becomes to see miracles in my life. When my family started asking *what*, we were propelled to move first to Memphis then to St. Louis. These places offered deaf schools that were paramount in Noah's development at an early age. We returned to North Mississippi at the start of his fifth year of primary school. In the spring of 2014 Noah finished his sophomore year at Corinth High School and lettered on the varsity baseball team—while maintaining a 3.75 grade-point-average. His accomplishments in the hearing world did not happen in an instant but that makes it no less a miracle.

Why doesn't God give us a miracle? No more asking! He gives them to us every day. There are just some who are more skilled at seeing them, like Chucky. He was willing to look past what he didn't have—into what he did have. For years, Chucky Mullins provoked in me the following question: *Why did he smile?* The journey of writing the book has me asking, *How can I not smile, with a teacher like him to inspire me?*

34: LOSS

CHUCKY MULLINS WAS PREPARING FOR CLASS ON WEDNESDAY, MAY 1, 1991, when tragedy struck him in his Oxford, Mississippi home. He suddenly stopped breathing and lost consciousness shortly thereafter. He was transported to the Oxford Hospital and later airlifted to Memphis, Tennessee. It was determined by the medical professionals that a previously undetected blood clot had traveled to Chucky's lungs, leaving him unable to breathe. He died on Monday, May 6, 1991, at the Baptist Memorial Hospital in Memphis.

Jeff Carter was a member of the 1991 Ole Miss Rebels Football team. A standout quarterback at Central High School in Tuscaloosa, Alabama, Carter was passed up by his hometown Crimson Tide. He walked-on at Ole Miss and, against all odds, eventually won the starting position at free safety. Now, during his senior season, Carter was selected as the second person to wear Number 38 on Chucky's behalf. But just a few months after Chucky's death, Carter became the first Rebel to wear 38 in his teammate's memory, rather than his honor.

On November 16th of that season the Rebels arrived in Knoxville, Tennessee, treading water to keep their bowl hopes afloat. They would need a victory in one of these last two games to preserve a winning season.

Coach Billy "Dog" Brewer gave a moving pre-game speech and the players finished their prayer. They now rose in unison and headed toward the field of battle. Prior to reaching the exit, Jeff Carter stepped in front of his teammates and took the floor.

Carter raised his right arm high into the air and yelled, "I have a 3 on this arm." He then lifted his left arm so that both fists pointed, parallel, to the heavens. Now, with his voice raised to a fever pitch he continued, "And on this arm I have an 8." He then crossed his arms in front of his face in the formation of a V. "When you put the 3 and 8 together you get victory!" He said, his voice exploding with emotion.

It was a moving speech and Carter roused the team with his passion. But the emotions of the moment lacked a sixty-minute impact on the players. When the clock hit its final tick, the Rebels experienced their fifth *loss* of the season.

Ole Miss finished the season with a losing record of 5-6 and would not go to a bowl in 1991. It appeared to some that the Rebels had played with no heart that year. But, the truth is, they played valiantly with heavy hearts.

After his injury, Chucky became a teacher of how to respond to extreme adversity with a winning attitude. Now his teammates, and everyone who loved him, were grieving the *loss* of their instructor. Chucky's death affected the Rebels *on the field* more than the fans could understand. And the pain touched the players *off the field* at the inner depths of their young souls.

It is my hope that the lasting memory of Chucky Mullins is not of one who died, but of a young man who taught so many how to live with character, courage, determination, grace, positivity, love, friendship, and a smile.

With a quick glance, it appears that Chucky's life ended in a *loss* when the final horn sounded. But if we cast our gaze upon his existence from an eternal view, we can see that he was merely behind when time ran out. True victory is not only determined by the final score but also by how we play the game and the lasting effect of our efforts. Yes, he lost the temporary battle with paralysis on earth, but he now knows the permanent victory as a restored child of God.

Jeff Carter gave the *Victory* speech against Tennessee, but the Rebels didn't win. Despite the defeat, the words of Carter rang prophetically. The victory of the 3 and the 8 can be found even in a *loss*. I am sad that Chucky died, but I am grateful that he is no longer restrained by his paralysis. My faith inspires me to believe that he is now living with a joy that we cannot currently fathom. While here on earth, he taught others how to live in victory, even in the face of death and defeat. He was indeed a consummate winner in a world filled with *loss*.

35: FEAR

ON SEPTEMBER 24, 2011, THE OLE MISS REBELS FOOTBALL TEAM WAS playing its fourth game of the season and desperately treading water to keep their ship afloat. They began the 2011 campaign with hopes of a significant improvement from the 4-8 record of 2010. But they soon found themselves in turbulent waters as they had lost two of their first three games. On this day, the Georgia Bulldogs were in town with no intentions of offering respite for their dismal beginning. When the final horn sounded, the Dawgs from Georgia prevailed, 27-13. The Rebels did not right the course and continued in the wrong direction, finishing the season 2-10.

Drew Meisenheimer was now 31 years old, and his life was still influenced by Chucky Mullins. Sure, he wanted to win as much as the next Rebels fan, but he also carried with him the perspective gained from his personal experience with Chucky's paralysis. Drew had learned to view a loss as if it were not the end of the world. Chucky had taught Drew that by approaching the bleakest challenge of his life—with a smile.

When the Rebels' season ended, by all accounts, with their defeat by Georgia, Drew was facing a much darker loss. Three weeks prior, his wife, Kate, had developed complications in her eighteenth week of pregnancy with twins. A visit to her physician would divulge a diagnosis of Twin-to-Twin Transfusion Syndrome (TTTS). TTTS is a condition in which blood passes unequally between identical twins who share a common placenta. When this transpires in early pregnancy, prior to twenty-six weeks, the fetuses have a high risk of death or being born with severe disabilities. Two weeks after the medical pronouncement, the young couple traveled to Cincinnati, Ohio, to attempt corrective surgery. Within a few days of the procedure, it would prove to have been ineffective.

Now, on the day of the fourth game of 2011, Kate was going into labor after only twenty-one weeks of pregnancy. Rather than Drew watching Ole Miss and Georgia on the gridiron, he was witnessing his twins' battle for life, along with the assistance of their brave mom. As the doctor approached the expectant dad, his expression delivered the grim news before he uttered a word. The babies would not prevail against the overwhelming odds that they faced.

At 10:11 a.m. Kate delivered the first of two still-born boys. Though the boys never drew a breath, they had been born, and deserved a name. The parents decided that each of them would choose a name for their sons. Kate chose the name Patrick Hastings in honor of her grandfather and grandmother. When it came time for Drew, his voice cracked as he uttered his namesake. The nurse asked, "I am sorry, sir, did you say Muller?"

Drew paused, took a deep breath, regained himself, and tried to begin again with a stronger voice, "M-U-L-L-I-N-S."

Kate now said what her husband could not, "It's pronounced Mullins."

In the fall of 1989, Chucky Mullins once shared that he was scared to go to sleep because he was afraid he would not wake up. To me, this is not a sign of weakness but a symbol of Chucky's humanity. Sure, he was afraid of dying at times because he loved living so much. But it is also important to understand that Chucky did not allow *fear* to take over his life. In other words, he didn't simply *exist* in *fear* after the accident; he continued to *live* in *joy*. That is what made all the difference in how he approached the world and changed it for the better.

It was that spirit that most inspired Drew and encouraged him to keep living after the immense tragedy that he had experienced. His football hero died when he was a star-struck kid. He had suffered through the pain that cancer plunged into him by assaulting his mom's life. And Drew experienced the deepest grief of any parent: the death of their children. As Drew endured these tragedies, it seems that Chucky not only taught Drew how to live but also how to face death. Like his hero, he refused to be conquered by *fear*.

It is May 6, 2013, and it has been eighteen months since Drew tragically lost his sons. He will celebrate his thirty-third birthday the next day and is feeling upbeat and reflective on the eve of his special day. The Ole Miss football team is on the upswing. They have just celebrated their most prestigious recruiting class of all time. The prior fall they played in their first bowl game in three years. The Rebels turnaround was a reminder to Drew that the losses and hard times we face in this life do not last forever. But football wasn't the real victory that he was considering on this evening.

He wrote the following text message to a family member as the night was about to end. "Twenty-two years ago tonight, my friend and hero Chucky Mullins died. This will always be a season of sadness and celebration for me—Chucky's death and my birth. I lost my twins eighteen months ago, and they are now with him in heaven. Through my pain, I am comforted knowing that Chucky is watching after them until I see them all again."

This is the world we live in: our teams lose and then they win. We know the pain of death and brokenness and the joy of life and healing. Drew has embraced Chucky's peace of knowing that there is something beyond this life. I suspect that Chucky is indeed looking after the Meisenheimer twins in heaven. No doubt teaching them to smile, while his memory gives their dad more to smile about on earth.

36: PURPOSE

IN THE SPRING OF 1992, MOLLY MEISENHEIMER'S BATTLE WITH CAN-
cer was over. Dr. Gruff had given a prognosis that she could have
less than two years to live. More accurately...life ended as she knew
it and began again. They didn't call it remission; it was far too early
for that. But twenty-four months after detection, Molly was finished with treatments completely.

Shortly after finishing the treatments in 1992, Molly began another battle. Cancer had thrown the first punch, and she beat it. She
was now inspired to pick another fight with breast cancer. However,
this brawl would be on behalf of her sisters the world over. Molly reasoned, "I was fortunate to have insurance and family support. Some
women are not that well-equipped to deal with this horrific disease.
I wanted to help them get through it."

She began working as a volunteer on behalf of a national breast
cancer organization. The charitable institution raised funds by con-
ducting running events in various cities throughout the nation.
Molly paid her own way to visit their headquarters and recruited
the organization to start a race in Memphis.

She would become the founder and chair of their first-ever race
in Memphis. She knew nothing of fund raising or what would be
involved with coordinating the event. Local running clubs told her
to expect around 250 participants the first year and that 500 would
be phenomenal.

Molly was an art teacher, not a professional fund-raiser. But she loved to talk and hated what cancer had done to so many. Her hair was just growing back from her own treatment. All the while, she went to work raising support and searching out runners.

Race day came and they had 1,753 runners! The next year they doubled the runners to over 3,000. By the third year, they were a series force and doubled their participants again to over 6,000. The race continued to garner success throughout the eight years she served as the chair. The total number of runners for the last event she served as chair had 13,500 runners.

Along the way, she learned about the challenges that occur when one mingles sponsors who possess the same business model. Some sponsors demanded that they be the exclusive *"partner"* to represent their market area. Caught off-guard by this tactic initially, she gained the courage to rebuff their offers by saying, "Cancer does not *exclude* particular women. It happens to all women, those who are treated at your hospital, and your competitors. Women who have cancer go to your grocery store as well as your competition's."

Several years into the race, Molly was asked by a national retailer to allow it exclusive sponsorship in exchange for $100,000 of support. This would have required her dissolving the relationship with the very first sponsor to commit to the race at its inception. She walked out of their posh boardroom to gather her thoughts at the enormity of the offer. A few minutes later, she re-entered with these words: "I'm just a small-town girl from Selmer, Tennessee. I am honored to receive such a huge offer from your company. But right now, I am remembering what my Momma and Daddy taught me, *"Always go home with the one who took you to the dance."* With that, Molly gathered her papers and her outfit-matching purse. She thanked them for their time and walked out on their offer.

Some would say that Molly made a bad business decision that

day. But coupled with her passion to raise funds was a burning desire to do it the right way. She kept plugging along the *right* way and secured more support to replace any that she lost. To date, she is personally responsible for raising over two million dollars to fight breast cancer—pretty good results for a small-town girl from Selmer, Tennessee.

In 2014, I visited with Molly in her home. She showed me a picture of Chucky Mullins that she and Ed still have prominently displayed in their kitchen. She became emotional while explaining her affection for Chucky. "I wish I had never gotten cancer, but I love the person I have become because of it. I wish Chucky had never suffered that injury. But what Chucky did for me and so many more…that was his *purpose* for living."

Chucky Mullins was not the sole source of encouragement for Molly Meisenheimer as she journeyed through the bleakest passages of her life. Her parents, Bill and Tommye Webb, gave her the best childhood that she could have asked for, and they were her rocks as she battled cancer. Her Sunday school class at Germantown United Methodist Church brought dinner three nights a week throughout her treatment process. There were other cancer patients, like a little gentleman named Bill Oakley, who always kept her spirits high.

To be sure, Chucky was not the sole reason why Molly survived cancer or raised $2 million for charity. But Molly would tell me that because Chucky lived his short, precious life with *purpose*, she was encouraged to make more *purpose* out of the *whys* that she faced. I'm not sure we will ever be able to fully quantify the wealth of contributions Chucky made upon this earth. He left an eternal legacy that continues to live beyond the lines of a football field. He may not have suffered his injury on *purpose*, but he gave *purpose* to many who witnessed his character.

Just prior to this book being published I received an early morning text message from someone who has become a dear friend, saying, "Today is the 24th anniversary of my biopsy! Love ya, Molly."

I don't think it is an accident that Molly keeps Chucky's picture displayed in her kitchen. I believe that this location was chosen on *purpose* as a symbol of how Chucky continues to nourish the souls and spirits of the entire Meisenheimer clan.

37: GRACE

PRIOR TO LEAVING THE PHILLIPS HOME BEFORE REPORTING TO OLE Miss his freshman year, Chucky gathered with the family for one last meal. Once everyone had finished eating, Chucky rose from the table and began washing the dishes. He had made a habit of performing this chore on many occasions. Karen would tell him not to bother but he would respond with a funny rebuttal and continue with his hands in the soapy water. Carver remembers with a laugh, "I think he did it so he could eat up all the leftovers after everybody else had left the kitchen."

But I suspect there was another reason Chucky displayed this caring gesture to the Phillips household. He was grateful for the home he had been given, and he wanted to contribute to the larger family. In essence, it was a symbolic offering of love shared by Chucky. Some call such a gift, *grace*.

For those who knew him well, the word *grace* personifies the nature of Chucky Mullins. It was this characteristic of his that inspired me to embark upon the adventure of this book with a central question: *How did Chucky respond to such extreme adversities in life with an abundance of grace?*

The passage through these pages has borne witness to grand accomplishments of people who have been inspired by Chucky's *grace*. Barriers that separate people along lines of race, class, and economic status have been challenged. Millions, yes, millions have been raised to fight cancer and provide assistance to victims of paralysis. Player safety in the sport of football has reached an awareness never acknowledged before. Countless academic scholarships have been awarded to assist people in need. Football coaches, players, fans, friends, and strangers have been inspired to live life more fully as a result of Chucky Mullins' effect on their lives.

In addition to the accomplishments that have been achieved by others, there is Chucky's direct personal impact to consider. Here are some of the gifts of *grace* that Chucky shared with the world: Inspiration, empowerment, forgiveness, courage, determination, humility, positivity, joy, purpose, thanksgiving, giver, receiver, conqueror, friend, worker, and hero. Most of all, he embodied these three tenets of a full life: faith, hope, and love.

As we consider the enormity of the gifts that Chucky lavished upon so many, I ask again: *How did Chucky respond to extreme adversity in life with such grace?*

I have come to believe that before Chucky gave grace, he received grace in an abundant portion. It seems that God equipped Chucky with an extra measure of *grace* to accompany his life's journey. Perhaps Chucky had a profusion of God's strength and comfort poured into him at birth. In the words of *Charity Bowl* founder Bill Courtney, "It was just in him!"

Thus I believe that God prepared Chucky for the challenges of his injury. This is not to say that God made Chucky get hurt, but as always, God had a holy knowing. With that knowing, the Lord clothed one of His precious creations with an extra gift of love and holiness called *grace*.

So with the dishes dried and put away, Chucky began preparing his things for the departure to Oxford, Mississippi, the next day. He arrived on campus with thirty other freshmen, prior to the varsity, in the summer of 1988.

Strength and conditioning coach Chuck Okey had sent us

workout material to begin performing prior to our arrival. But none of us were prepared for the grueling taxation upon our young bodies. The heat was overwhelming, and none of us had ever worked so hard on a football field. For most of us the curfew instituted by the coaches was an unnecessary requirement. We fell into the bed from exhaustion as soon as we finished the evening meal on most days.

Chucky's roommate, Derrick King, reflects on that first summer practice. "I won't ever forget Chucky and Tony Harris wrestling every morning in our room before practice. I would just shake my head and laugh. I was trying to conserve every ounce of energy that I had, getting ready for that blazing heat. Those dudes went at it every morning. I don't know where they found the energy."

Trea Southerland has similar memories about Chucky. "It seemed like he never got tired. He would hang out in your room as late as you would let him. I remember running him out on more than one occasion so I could go to sleep. It seemed like he had an extra gear that the rest of us were not equipped with."

Could the limitless energy Chucky's teammates witnessed be a symbol of the strength he had been given from above. Is it too much to believe that God would pour a little extra *grace* upon those who need it most in this life? The Apostle Paul didn't think so as he described his gift to the early Christian Church at Corinth. "But whatever I am now, it is all because God poured out his special favor on me—and not without results. For I have worked harder than any of the others; yet it was not I but God who was working through me by his *grace*." (1 Corinthians 15:10)

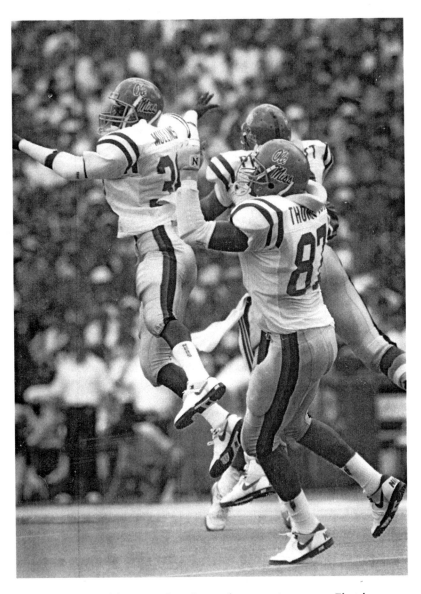

*Chucky celebrating a big play in the upset victory over Florida
with Keith Thompson and Kelvin Pritchett*

38

ON DECEMBER 31, 1992, THE FRESHMAN CLASS OF 1988 PLAYED OUR last football game for the Ole Miss Rebels. Had Chucky Mullins not sustained his injury and premature death, he would have been there with us playing in his last college football game as well. Time had passed, but his impact and memory had not faded from his teammates or the Ole Miss community.

On this evening, we defeated the Air Force Academy for the second time in three years while competing at the Liberty Bowl in Memphis, Tennessee. We won 31 games in four years and played in three post-season bowl games. Those accomplishments made us the winningest senior class in the prior twenty years of Ole Miss football.

With less than a minute to play on the game clock there was a delay in the on-field action for several minutes. I happened to be standing near head coach Billy Brewer as the post-game celebration was starting a little early on the sidelines. The delay had been long enough to become a bit of annoyance to our celebration. I looked up to the game clock to see how much time remained in the contest. The game clock was frozen with 38 seconds left to play. I pointed to the clock and said to our leader, "Coach, look how much time is on the clock."

The lines in his face were now pronounced as he had aged dramatically in the three years since Chucky's paralysis "38, kid! He's here, He's right here with us," Coach Brewer said with a smile.

As if choreographed by a skilled director, each player seemed to recognize the game clock simultaneously. Someone began an impromptu chant that started to reverberate all along the sideline, "Chucky, Chucky, Chucky..."

This was not the first occasion that Chucky's presence had been felt that season. In the fall of that year, on the first day of full contact practice, the team was assembling in the locker room in preparation to hit the field. Chucky's locker had not been reassigned since his injury, a symbolic reminder that Number 38 was still a part of the team. He had begun the journey with us in 1988, and we were gonna finish it together.

Snake Williams was having trouble getting dressed because he could not find his shoulder pads. After checking with all of the usual suspects who might have hidden them, Snake enlisted the help of the equipment management staff. They searched throughout the field house, including the equipment storage room. The pads remained missing-in-action so the search continued in the locker room.

Each locker included a box that resembled a child's toy chest. Equipment could be thrown recklessly into this bin, giving the appearance of tidiness on the outside. Things had a way of getting lost in this dungeon of the locker, going undetected for months. A freshman equipment manager was given the task of searching each player's smelly cupboard. The fumes of shoulder pads and molded socks were locked in the safe-keeping of its own funk in the lower bowels of each box. The rookie manager was making quick work of the search as his nostrils were invaded with the disgust of each new aroma. He had inspected nearly forty lockers when he finally hit pay dirt. He found the shoulder pads for number 78 located in the locker belonging to Number 38. Had he not been a freshman, or perhaps in such a hurry, he would never have touched the sacred locker.

When Snake Williams was informed that his shoulder pads had

been found in the locker of his teammate and friend Chucky Mullins, he was overcome with uncontrollable emotions. He felt that it was no accident. He had a spiritual sensation that Chucky was trying to say something to him. Snake has a naturally soft voice but you could hear his wails throughout the locker room. The mind of this enormous man raced like a child's, *Is he telling me not to play or is he telling me to play good? Is he trying to let me know to be careful on the field or let it all hang out and have a great senior season?*

The message that day may not have been exclusively for Snake Williams, it could have been intended for the entire team. Perhaps it was Chucky trying to communicate that day, or it could have been a message from an even higher source: *never quit living in the courage of 38.*

In 2004, the University commissioned the sculpture of a bronze bust in the likeness of Chucky Mullins. Since that time it has been displayed in the south end zone where the Ole Miss football team enters the field of play. It sits atop a concrete pedestal where Chucky's quote to *Never Quit* is inscribed.

The Athletic Department invited Chucky's teammates to attend the 2004 unveiling of the sculpture. The ceremony took place during halftime of a football game, and the former teammates of Number 38 were escorted onto the field to be recognized. As we walked onto the sidelines, just prior to halftime, there was a delay in the on field action for several minutes. It was the first time we had gathered as a team since our last game 12 years prior, at the Liberty Bowl. Unaware of why the game had been delayed, we looked up at the scoreboard and, once again, the game clock read 38.

The Ole Miss Rebels are not the first people to hold the number 38 in high esteem. For the ancient Icelandic people the numeral symbolized unnatural bravery and courage. The number 38 was especially prominent in their Norse mythology writings, which date back to the 13th century. The valiant heroes of the Norse sagas embodied the character that the number signified as they served humankind for good. Most legendary tales were divided into 38 chapters, and the number often recurred throughout the stories. All along the fabled writings, the heroes would combat giants or other enemies in groups of 38.

Chucky Mullins has become, for many people, a hero, but not because he had otherworldly powers like the mythological characters from long ago. Rather, it was his willingness to continue fighting as a normal human being in the face of giant obstacles that has given inspiration to many.

As I close this book, we are approaching the 25th anniversary of Chucky's injury. This is an appropriate time for us to remember everything that Chucky Mullins gifted our world with at this historical occasion.

Maybe the message in the Ole Miss locker room that day in 1992 was not just for Snake Williams. I suspect that it was not merely for the teammates assembled that day either. Perhaps the real meaning was a commission to us all: *Never quit living in the courage of 38.*

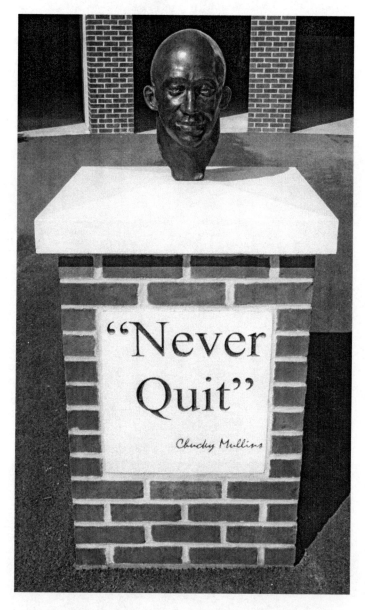

The Chucky Mullins bust that the Ole Miss Football team touches
before entering the field of play before each home game

ACKNOWLEDGEMENTS

MY WIFE MONYA, ALONG WITH MY SONS NOAH AND LUKE HAVE BEEN extremely supportive of me throughout the journey with this book. I am blessed to share my life with them and will always be grateful for their contribution to my life's joy.

My parents, Gerald and Sherry Hill, have provided wisdom and insight to this process as they have to every part of my life. I could not have asked for more loving and nurturing parents.

Charlie and Martha Spearman welcomed me into their family twenty years ago. Thank you for gifting me with your daughter.

Carver and Karen Phillips are the life blood of this book. Simply stated, there would be no book without their involvement. They provided me with personal information about Chucky that I could have never attained without them.

Molly Meisenheimer opened her life's book to me and shared the extraordinary story of their family. In addition, she assisted in every way that she could and inspired me all along the way.

Author Margaret King was tireless in her efforts as the primary editor of this book. She is one of the most giving people that I have ever had the fortune of knowing. I will never be able to repay her for the vast wealth of contribution.

Author Katherine King has been a great source of encouragement. I am grateful to call her, and twin sister Margaret, my friends as they made this process more fulfilling.

My new friends at Deeds Publishing were a joy to work with and were patient with me as a novice writer. Thank you Bob, Mark and Jan.

There are five friends who went beyond my expectations and this book would not have been the same without them. My words limit the depth of appreciation I have for the contribution of Orma Smith, Scott Swatzell, Reeca Lockhart Elliott, Deano Orr, and Shawn Cobb.

Coach Billy Brewer and Cooper Manning both embody Ole Miss Royalty in my mind. I will be eternally grateful for their willingness to give credence to this book and me personally.

University of Mississippi Chancellor Dr. Dan Jones gave me an audience to introduce the books concept and offered his support. Ole Miss Athletic Director Ross Bjork is a gift to our University and exceeded my imagination in his willingness to assist the telling of Chucky's story. Here are others in the Ole Miss community that poured life into this project: Langston Rogers, Leroy Mullins, Chuck Okey, Chuck Rounsaville, Bill Courtney, Dr. Tom Eppes, Keith Carter, Michael Thompson, Micah Ginn, Clay Cavett, Col. Florian-Jesse Yoste, Carey Freeze and David Kellum.

My following Ole Miss teammates provided me interview time and filled in some spaces in my memory of our beloved Chucky: Scott Swatzell, Shawn Cobb, Deano Orr, Chris "Creek" Mitchell, Jeff Carter, Trea Southerland, Sebastian "Snake" Williams, Louis Gordon, Jay Hopson, Derrick King, Tom Luke, Jack Muirhead, Clint Conlee, Abner White, Derek Jones, Jim McCay, Stu Anderson, Todd Sandroni, and John Darnell.

Chucky's family and friends from the Russellville, Alabama area were vital in providing details of his early life. Horace Mullins, Dorothy Mullins, Coach Don Cox, Aleshia Phillips, Keshia Phillips Sears, Lamar Phillips, Ramono Craig, Wade Sumerel, Tommy James, Deedra Seale Moore, Mrs. Betty Sibley, Coach Ted Ikerd,

Coach Butch Hartness, Joe Cooper, Bobby Winston and Kellie Singleton.

The following family and friends gave me valuable support to make this book a reality. Ripley Presbyterian Church, Price Elliott, Judge Bobby Elliott, Fred Permenter Jr., Charles Davis, Jimmy Hill, Kenny Hill, Lynn Hill, Bobby Martin, Dr. Carol Livingston, Rev. Dr. Don Elliott, Rev. Dr. Ronald Meeks, Rev. Dr. Jay Earheart-Brown, Rev. Dr. Bob Rambo, Pastor Mike Boles, Sis. Clare Van Lent, Sis. Mary Horrell, Clint McClamroch, Dr. Pat Tucker, Randy Long, Pat Palmer, Trey Albright, Stuart Green, Ricky James, Greg Williams, Chet Dickson, Diane Dickson, Brandon Vance, Susan Vance and Scott Green.

There are some people that I did not know before writing this book but they contributed to its success. My life and this book has been enriched by these individuals. Brad Gaines, Angela Hammond, Jason Jones, Deterrian Shackelford, Matt Wyatt, Ed Meisenheimer, Drew Meisenheimer, Kate Meisenheimer, Tyler Meisenheimer, Lindsey Meisenheimer, Coach Curley Hallman, Lyn Roberts, Richard Howorth, Caitlin Adams and Margaret Bell.

Finally, but most of all I am most grateful to God. I pray that this book will inspire His people and glorify His name.

SOURCES

I AM ESPECIALLY INDEBTED TO THE CREATIVE STIMULATION PROVID-ed by the following three prior works on Chucky Mullins. *A Dixie Farewell: The Life and Death of Chucky Mullins* by Larry Woody; *Undefeated: The Chucky Mullins Story*, a documentary directed and produced by Micah Ginn; *Against the Grain: A Coach's Wisdom on Character, Faith, Family, and Love* by Bill Courtney.

The following writers provided valiant coverage of Chucky Mullins in the years surrounding his injury. I gained knowledge from their work and would like to recognize each one: Don Whitten, Raad Cawthon, Jeremy S. Weldon, Mike Knobler, Randy Kenner, Mike Fleming, James Chisum, Gene Phelps, Al Dunning, Amy Vincent, Rick Cleveland, Bill Courtney, Mary Nettleton, Tara Hart, Denton Gibbes, Sonya Mason, Kate Magandy, Christi Townsend, Amy Stewart, Bobby Hall, John Branston, and Jimmie Covington.

ABOUT THE AUTHOR

JODY HILL WAS BORN IN FALKNER, Mississippi. In the fall of 1988, he became friends with Chucky Mullins when they were freshmen on the Ole Miss Rebels football team. He became a 1992 graduate of the University of Mississippi. In 2000, Jody earned a Master of Divinity degree from the Memphis Theological Seminary and was ordained into Christian ministry by the Cumberland Presbyterian Church of Memphis, Tennessee. He lives in Corinth, Mississippi, with his wife, Monya, and two sons, Noah and Luke. To schedule an appearance visit: www.RevJodyHill.com.

DEDICATION

This book is dedicated to former Ole Miss Head Football Coach Billy Brewer, his coaches, support staff and players of the 1989 Ole Miss Rebels Football Team.

1989 Coaches and Staff: Billy Brewer, Warner Alford, Jody Allen, Blake Barnes, Bonnie Bishop, Gunter Brewer, Willie Buford, Reed Davis, Larry Dorsey, Chuck Driesbach, Andy Friedlander, Keith Garner, Virginia Hall, Robert Henry, Mark Hovanic, Max Howell, Art Kaufman, Alan Loller, Scott McKinney, Pat Milligan, Leroy Mullins, Chuck Okey, Red Parker, Debra Patterson, Rick Petri, Jim Rieves, Langston Rogers, Jeff Sarver, James "T" Thomas, Robert Thompson, Joe Wickline and Mike Zullo.

1989 Student Managers: Chris Ayers, Scotty Mitchell, Greg Murphey, Randy Parrish, John Ross, Mike Shoemaker, Damon Stroud, Brent Travis and Chad Vega.

1989 Student Trainers: Andrew Boyd, Andy Dalton, David Estes, David Ferguson, Spence Fletcher, Pam Kincaid, Jeff Moore, Tim Mullins, Jannell Replogle, Lynnette Schwarrtz (GA), Steve Thompson and Michael Todd Winter.

1989 Football Players: Gary Abide, Dwayne Amos, Perry Arrington, Tyrone Ashley, Randy Baldwin, Chris Battiste, Tony Bennett, Darron Billings, Vince Bonham, Danny Boyd, Scott Bratton, Burkes Brown, Glenn Brown, Tim Brown, Tony Brown, Bill Bush, Brian Cagle, Handy Campbell, Herky Cantu, Jeff Carter, Charles Childers, Sherwood Cobarras, Shawn Cobb, Pat Coleman, Clint Conlee, Marvin Courtney, Roy Dampier, John Darnell, Ben David, Steve Davis, Cliff Dew, Mike Easton, Rich Gebbia, Chauncey Godwin, Louis Gordon, Willie Green, Bubba Gunter, Roger Hancock, David Harris, Pete Harris, David Herring, Tony Hervey, Devin Hickerson, Jody Hill, Reid Hines, Greg Hogue, Jeff Holder, Jay Hopson, Doug Jacobs, Scott Jerome, Glen Jones, Kenny Jones, Joel Jordan, Phillip Kent, Derrick King, Brian Lee, Jim Lentz, Victor Lester, Everett Lindsay, Dameion Logan, Lee Lott, Tom Luke, Brian Mays, Gerald McAllister, Jim McCay, Ronnie McKinney, Thomas McLeish, Mike Mears, Wesley Melton, Chris "Creek" Mitchell, John Moore, Wayne Muckle, Jack Muirhead, Chucky Mullins, Sean O'Malley, Deano Orr, Reggie Parrott, Paul Pennington, Monty Perry, Don Price, Kelvin Pritchett, Dawson Pruett, Jeff Rhodes, Ricky Richardson, Camp Roberts, Michael Robinson, Todd Sandroni, Brian Schnitta, Maurice Shaw, Russ Shows, Darryl Smith, Mac Smith, Trea Southerland, Mike Sparks, Monty Spencer, Rogers Stephens, Brad Stevens, Adrian Strother, Frank Sullivan, Scott Swatzell, Ed Thigpen, Jim Earl Thomas, Keith Thompson, Nate Thornton, Clay Vann, Gerald Vaughn, J.J. Walker, Greg Watson, Dan Westmoreland, Abner White, Josh White, Dan Wigley, Clint Wilcke, Michael Wilkerson, Ken Williams, Sebastian "Snake" Williams, Deron Zeppelin.

CPSIA information can be obtained at www.ICGtesting.com
Printed in the USA
BVOW03s0412071114

373745BV00008B/229/P